GOTH

THIS IS A CARLTON BOOK

This edition published in 2016 by Carlton
Books Limited
20 Mortimer Street
London W1T 3JW

First published in hardback in 2014 by
Goodman

10 9 8 7 6 5 4 3 2 1

Text and Design © Carlton Publishing Group
2014, 2016

A CIP catalogue record for this book is
available from the British Library.

ISBN 978 1 78097 886 4

Printed in China

Senior Executive Editor: Lisa Dyer
Managing Art Editor: Mabel Chan
Picture Researcher: Emma Copestake
Production Manager: Maria Petalidou

PREVIOUS PAGE

Gareth Pugh, Spring/
Summer 2012.

RIGHT

Promotional poster for
The Woman in Black
(2012).

OVERLEAF

Silent-screen actress
Theda Bara.

WHAT DID THEY SEE?

FEBRUARY 2012
WOMANINBLACK.COM

© 2011 CBS FILMS INC.

GOTH

THE DESIGN, ART AND FASHION OF A DARK SUBCULTURE

CHRIS ROBERTS

HYWEL LIVINGSTONE

EMMA BAXTER-WRIGHT

CARLTON BOOKS

Contents

"All that we see or seem is
but a dream within a dream."

Edgar Allan Poe

INTRODUCTION: PRETTY CHILLS

In truth, "Gothic" isn't one of those words that means all things to all people. To most today, it instantly evokes an oft-caricatured spookiness; chills and thrills inspired by Morticia Addams and Bela Lugosi and aligned with morose dark garb. Yet the long history of the term shows it has survived and evolved – undead, if you will – over centuries, embracing in various eras both an anti-establishment sense of subversion and a florid, fevered, fashion-statement twist on camp. From its roots – the Goths, an ancient Germanic people who resisted the Roman Empire – through a style tribe that enjoyed an aesthetic penchant for black and a literary movement which still conjures up images of bats flitting across a full moon and distracted women stumbling through ancient, gargoyle-garnished ruins while fleeing sinister figures in long black cloaks hover behind tombstones, it has represented a "danse macabre". It has also stood strong and reached high as an ambitious architectural style, a genre of underground rock music and a distinctive visual aesthetic, adopted within both fashion and the visual arts. Appropriately, the gothic has proven remarkably durable and adaptable, endlessly reimagining itself across time, and now as fertile and vital as ever. In the twenty-first century, its morbid preoccupations are perceived as sexy as much as scary, glamorous as much as gloomy. Its dark heart beats to its own rhythms: cult yet commercial, transgressive yet topical.

This book examines its backstory and celebrates its pulsating present. Although there must necessarily remain an element of the unknown about the gothic, we can psalm its icons and probe its intrigues. There is so much more to it than the clichés: it is rich and contains multitudes. From Hieronymus Bosch to the Chapman Brothers, from the Houses of Parliament to Lincoln Cathedral, from H.P. Lovecraft to Edgar Allan Poe, from *Nosferatu* to *The Wicker Man*, from the flamboyant dandy to the denizens of the Batcave, from Theda Bara to Alexander McQueen, from Joy Division to Marilyn Manson, the gothic has tales aplenty to whisper in your ear. Perhaps with what Stephen King, eulogizing Lovecraft, called "the voice whispering from inside the pillow".

So sit in the shadow of St Vitus Cathedral in Prague, don your finest black velvet and lace, ponder *The Lady of Shalott* and *Suspiria* while reading *The Castle of Otranto* and listening to *A Kiss in the Dreamhouse* – and wallow and rejoice in the very human condition known as "Gothic". In the 1935 film *Bride of Frankenstein*, Byron speaks of the "pretty chills" of Mary Shelley. Seduce your darkest demons and shiver in a kind of ecstasy at their beauty.

PREVIOUS PAGE
American Gothic *(1930) by Grant Wood. Originally based on the setting of a Gothic Revival farmhouse in Iowa, the painting is often described as a mourning portrait with its sombre figures and curtain-drawn windows. It is one of the most recognized paintings in twentieth-century American art.*

OPPOSITE
A memento mori from Hans Memling's triptych Earthly Vanity and Divine Salvation *(c.1485).*

"The oldest and strongest emotion of mankind is fear, and the oldest and strongest kind of fear is fear of the unknown."

H. P. Lovecraft

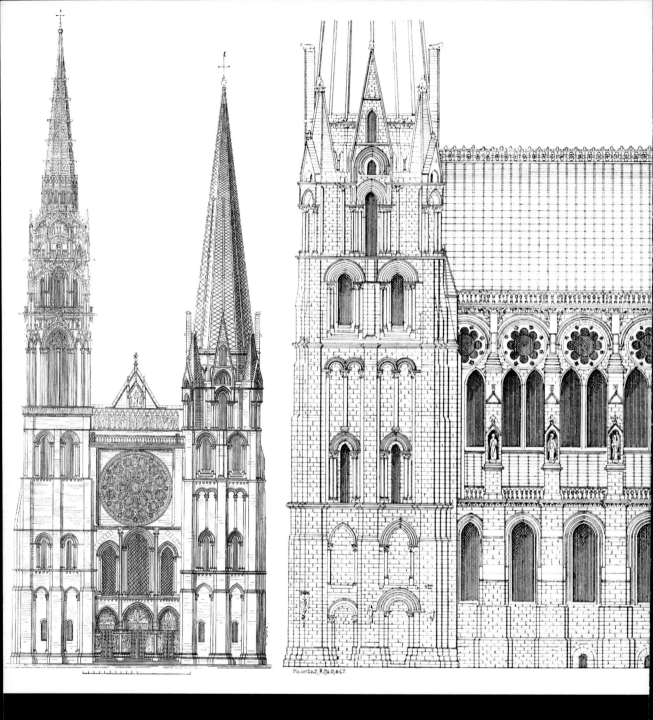

"The principle of the Gothic architecture is infinity made imaginable."

Samuel Taylor Coleridge

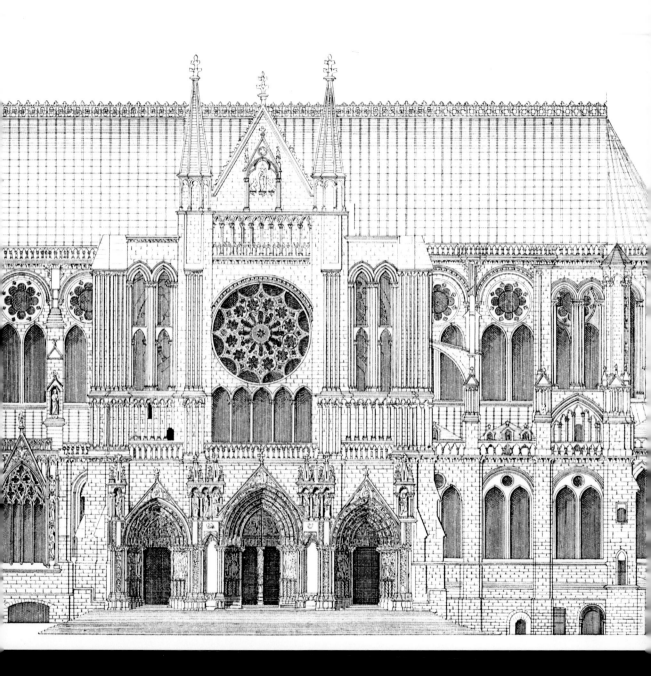

ARCHITECTURE

WE CAN STATE with some confidence that the fountainhead of all that was to follow in the rich and diverse (and sometimes tenuous) world of the gothic aesthetic was Gothic architecture. As with most historical "isms" and movements, a retrospective quip gave us the title, and an accumulation of scholarly sparring over subsequent generations gave us the content. Horrified by the lack of classical principles present in contemporary buildings, Italian architectural writers in the fifteenth century (undoubtedly caught up in the fervour of the Renaissance with its revolutionary approach to optics, vision and perspective) quite naturally deemed the buildings around them irrelevant, vulgar and overpowering. What better term to name them than that of the marauding hoards who, like the architecture that so offended the sensitive Italians, ruined their beloved Rome back in the fifth century?

An architectural theme that followers of gothic sensibilities would be familiar with is the disregard for rules and convention. This may sound absurd to the contemporary viewer of medieval architecture, but when compared to their classical predecessors, Gothic buildings (and in particular cathedrals) did not follow a rigorous and predetermined rule book. The proportion, geometry and order that was so essential to classical buildings was replaced with a far more metaphysical desire to build an evocation of the heavenly Jerusalem on earth. The motive was to create a space that provided a stage for spectacular ceremony and visual wonder, to encourage and accommodate movement and sound demanded by the liturgy, and to display secular wealth. With ego, piety and money dictating the outcome, as opposed to structured rules and convention, the results are, even today, awe-inspiring.

PREVIOUS PAGE

This architectural drawing of the thirteenth-century cathedral of Chartres in France epitomizes what has latterly become known as High Gothic. Comparing the cathedral against the original drawings demonstrates a rare example of master masons adhering to their architect's plans.

OPPOSITE

Built in the 1240s as a home for relics of Christ's Passion, the Saint Chapelle encapsulates not only architectural grandeur, but the stunning ornamentation associated with Gothic cathedrals.

RIGHT

Showing a depiction of the celebration of Christmas Mass at Sainte Chapelle in Paris, this early fifteenth-century illuminated manuscript by the Limburg Brothers reflects in its composition the architectural motifs of the Gothic cathedral, with the position of the three monks at the altar leading the eye upward.

Abbot Suger and the Royal Abbey of St Denis

The Royal Abbey of St Denis in Paris is broadly acknowledged as being the first, definitive example of Gothic architecture in its full and spectacular splendour. The site upon which the Abbey is founded was determined by the gloriously gothic legend of St Denis, the first bishop of Paris who walked to the spot freshly decapitated, carrying his own head. Abbot Suger (*c.*1081–1151), on his appointment to the abbey in 1124, began an enthusiastic campaign of commissioning new and dazzling reliquaries to house the precious relics that not only provided a direct link to heaven, but also a valuable source of income from visiting pilgrims. Due to the perennial conflict between church and state, France was at the time under threat from both the English King Henry I (1068–1135) and the Holy Roman Emperor Henry V (1086–1125). Having made a pious promise to God that if he was victorious he would endow France's patron saint with gifts and riches, Louis VI (1081–1137) took his troops to Reims ready to

BELOW

What better way to prove the authenticity of a legend than to claim possession of its gory aftermath? Part of St Denis' decapitated head is claimed to be held in the reliquary at the Royal Abbey of St Denis.

RIGHT

After being struck by lightning in 1837, the north tower of St Denis (on the left), was so badly damaged that it had to be demolished, never to be rebuilt.

fight the emperor. The emperor, in an apparent answer to the French king's prayers, withdrew and, true to his word, Louis afforded Abbot Suger the resources he required to fulfil his vision. Suger's instructions were both single-minded and structurally vague. The key demands were a suitably grand setting for the shrine of the patron saint, enough space for the visiting pilgrims to circulate and get a good view of the relic, and a huge amount of light – the purest and most direct evocation of heaven. The instructions to the architect drew on an interpretation of the divine taken form liturgical imagery, rather than any practical architectural rule. The simplest way to create more light was, of course, to create bigger windows. But more glass meant less stone, which meant less structural integrity. These problems formed the basis of what have become key signifiers of the Gothic architectural aesthetic – the removal of supporting walls to create more space, resulting in internal columns and ribbed vaulting, combined with external buttresses to cope with the incredible weight. Every structural aspect of the Gothic cathedral had a direct link to liturgical symbolism or function, from the cruciform shape of the building's footprint, to the great empty expanse of the knave built to accommodate the awestruck public, and the curved arches and vaulted windows symbolically evoking everlasting life. All this was in direct and conscious opposition to the austere finality of classical design. With each subsequent cathedral, the masons and their patrons competed to outdo the previous building, with the demand for more light producing ever larger and taller windows, resulting in more ingenious and gravity defying engineering.

ABOVE

The Royal Abbey of St Denis, Paris. Illuminated by huge windows, the enormous expanse of lateral and vertical space achieved by replacing supporting walls with columns gives the illusion that the vaulted ceiling is floating heavenward.

ABOVE

Bourges Cathedral, France (c.1195–1230). The addition of buttresses to the outside meant that the huge structural pressures could be externalized, supporting the weak points where the interior columns met and divided into the vaulted ceiling.

OPPOSITE

Chartres Cathedral, France (c.1145–1220). A common attribute among all Gothic cathedrals is the cruciform plan. The nave, where the public would gather, is longer than the other three arms.

The Gothic in England

It wasn't until 1174 that one of the finest examples of Gothic architecture emerged in England, after a blazing fire swept through and destroyed a large part of Canterbury Cathedral. But it was the dramatic events of four years before that inspired the eventual outcome of the cathedral's rebuild, with a gruesome turn of events that would prove to be worthy of any nineteenth-century gothic imagination. England's Archbishop Thomas Becket was charming, intelligent, well-connected and influential, and soon became chancellor to King Henry II (1133-1189). But instead of becoming a powerful double act, Thomas fell out with the king, abandoning his courtly duties for long bouts of prayer and solitude. Eventually he was forced into exile in France, where for seven years he practised austere piety. Becket returned in December 1170 having reinvented his public persona from political agitator to revered holy man, which only enraged the king further. As the tensions between the two began to mount, word spread of the

ABOVE

Canterbury Cathedral can be traced back to the seventh century, its sprawling architecture a record of a thousand years of religious conflict and political change.

LEFT

Canterbury Cathedral's East end (c.1179). The use of pink and white stone and marble was a stroke of genius by Sens' replacement, William of England, encapsulating the violent drama of Becket's death with emblematic significance.

BELOW

Depiction of the murder of Thomas Becket, stained glass window, Canterbury Cathedral. The cult of Thomas Becket spread around Europe extraordinarily quickly, forcing the Pope to declare him a saint in one of the fastest canonizations ever.

king's displeasure. Four barons decided to take direct action, and with a group of armed men set off to the cathedral, presumably to arrest Becket. There was a vehement verbal resistance from the forthright Becket and, with a crowd of spectators watching the confrontation, things got ugly. In the flurry of sword slashes and fists, Becket's skull was split open, and he fell to the ground. Blood and brains were spattered across the floor and upon seeing the gory result of their actions, the knights fled. Almost immediately the martyrdom of this holy man was acknowledged, and the opportunistic medieval onlookers dashed forward to daub their eyes with the blood – literally imbibing his body – while others dipped their clothes in the gore. The visual potency of the red and the white mingling on the floor was powerful in its symbolism, evoking the suffering of Christ himself. Soon enough the cult of Becket took hold, so that when the fire ruined the east end of the cathedral four years later it was seen as a perfect opportunity to finally do his martyrdom justice.

Wells Cathedral, England (1176–1490). The unusual scissor arch in the nave of Wells Cathedral distinguishes it from French architectural influence and displays an ingenious twist on the vaulted arch, evoking the link between heaven and earth.

OPPOSITE

Lincoln Cathedral, England (1074–1548). An excellent example of zealous piety dictating outcome, the so-called "crazy vault" ceiling of St Hughes choir is completely asymmetrical, leading the eye fervently along.

Much Like Abbot Suger's demands to create a platform to venerate St Denis, the rebuild of Canterbury Cathedral was wholly based around the martyrdom of Becket, and the desire to maximise both the impact of his sainthood and the revenue from visiting pilgrims. Master masons were sought out and interviewed, with William of Sens (bringing with him the skills and flair he'd displayed in the building of Sens Cathedral in France) winning the contract. One of the many notable introductions William made to English Gothic architecture was that of the fully exposed flying buttress, seen in the presbytery of the cathedral. William suffered a crippling fall from a scaffold in 1179 and was replaced by William of England, who took up the complex job of rebuilding by adding his own dramatic flourishes, such as building columns using rare pink and white marble – a direct reference to Becket's spilled blood and brains and a symbol of his virginity and martyrdom. Once again, drama, death and spirituality coupled with innovative and inspired individual craftsmanship dictated the outcome, resulting in a complex and often mind-boggling amalgamation of gothic features.

Late Gothic Architecture

Gothic architectural design rapidly spread, as did the ambition of the patrons and the skill of the architects. By the Late Gothic period between the latter years of the fourteenth century and the early years of the sixteenth century, magnificent examples of Gothic architecture were appearing all over Europe. One of the more notable cathedrals of this period is the Cathedral of St Vitus in the grounds of Prague Castle, Czech Republic. Charles IV (1316–78), King of Bohemia and Holy Roman Emperor, wanted to create a central European version of Paris, complete with its own university and magnificent cathedral. Keen to make a statement worthy of the power and prestige of Bohemia, Charles spared no expense, diverting ten percent of the enormous royal revenue generated by Bohemian silver mines to meet the cost of building the cathedral. In 1355 and at great cost, he purchased the relics of St Vitus, who was to become the patron saint of the cathedral. Work on building the cathedral was begun by the architect – personally recruited by the Emperor – Matthew of Arras (1290–1352). But it wasn't until Matthew died, with most of the work still incomplete, that St Vitus Cathedral was transformed into what has become one of the finest examples of central European late Gothic architecture. The mastermind behind the work was Peter Parler (c.1330–1399), who in 1356 was drafted in to replace his predecessor at the precocious age of twenty-three. Parler was from a family of prestigious architects, and was at the cutting edge of architectural development. He worked on the cathedral over the following sixty years or so, introducing beautiful details exemplified by the vaults above the sacristy. In a complex mirror image of the ribbed vaulting, the ribs themselves are drawn out three dimensionally and suspended, as if dropping back down to earth – a beautiful example of the advanced engineering and ingenuity displayed by Parler, pushing the boundaries of what was already a dramatic gothic trope.

Long after the completion of St Vitus Cathedral, and in the closing stages of the Gothic era between 1492 and 1502, King Vladislav II (1456–1516) reconstructed his castle in Prague on whose grounds the cathedral stands. Clearly influenced by the elaborate and intricate designs of Peter Parler, Vladislav's master mason Benedikt Ried (c.1450–1531) was able to knock through three large rooms to create one enormous throne room and jousting hall, the intricate ribbed ceiling curving down into the floor providing the structural support for the massive, 16-metre expanse.

OPPOSITE ABOVE

St Vitus Cathedral, Prague. The work of the young master mason Peter Parler proved to be as strong an influence on central European Gothic architecture as the Sainte Chapelle was in Paris.

OPPOSITE BELOW

Demonstrating technical virtuosity, the suspended vaults in the sacristy of St Vitus Cathedral showcase Parler's groundbreaking creative ambition.

RIGHT

Vladislav Hall, Prague Castle (1492–1502). Vladislav II needed a room large enough for coronations, banquets and matters of state. The biggest secular space in medieval Prague, it was even able to accommodate competing knights on horseback.

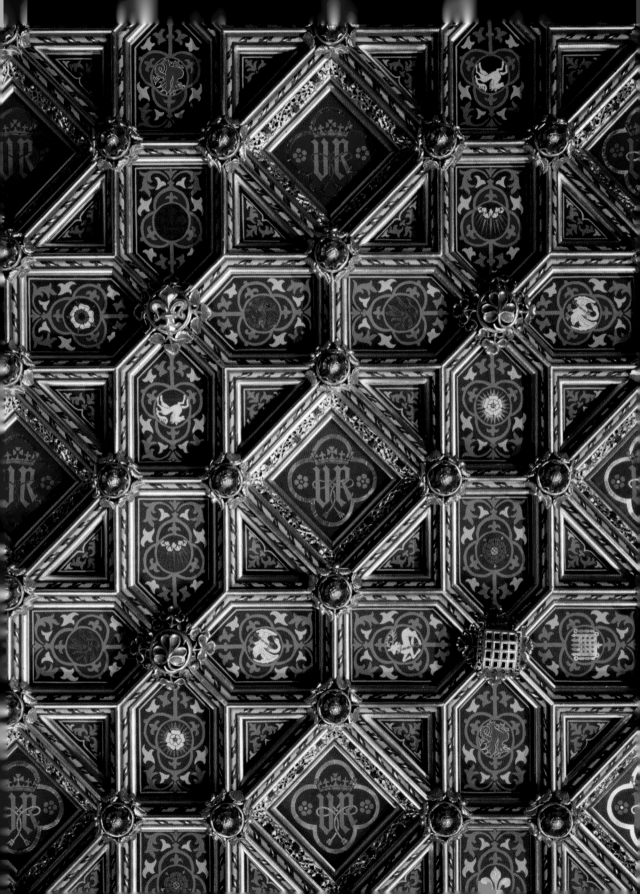

Gothic Revival Architecture

OPPOSITE

The ceiling of the Robing Room, designed by Pugin for the Palace of Westminster, is decorated with intricate panelling depicting badges of the monarchs of England, and is where the Queen puts on her robes of state before entering Parliament.

Proof of the powerful influence and longevity of Gothic architecture is its re-emergence in the mid-nineteenth century. Victorian Gothic Revival emerged not only as a way of creating symbolic and visually arresting buildings, both secular and religious, but also as a way of appropriating through visual association the high moral and Christian values that underpinned the original Gothic cathedrals. A fine example of this is the Palace of Westminster, London. After burning down in 1834, the Palace was redesigned by Sir Charles Barry (1795–1860) and A. W. N. Pugin (1812–52). Taking over thirty years to build, from 1836 to 1868, Barry and Pugin never saw its completion. Pugin was particularly instrumental in the outcome of the now iconic building, being responsible for the stylistic medieval design of the outer surfaces. Given a clean slate to re-build after the fire, the architects deemed it far more suitable to build to the design of Christian cathedrals rather than the alternative, the less suitable neo-classicism associated with pagan Greece.

LEFT

While Sir Charles Barry organized the rebuilding of the ruined Palace of Westminster, Augustus Pugin planned everything from the exterior decoration to the detailed interior surfaces, as shown in this geometrically complex watercolour-and-ink-wash ceiling design.

Pugin's beautiful designs went beyond the interior and exterior surfaces to include furniture, such as this large cabinet for the Palace of Westminster. The cabinet was displayed in the Great Exhibition of 1851, held in London to demonstrate to the world the skill and ingenuity of Britain's artists, designers and engineers, and was part of Pugin's display depicting the medieval court.

Houses of Parliament, London, England (1836–68). The revival of Gothic architecture was due to its Christian associations, favoured by nineteenth-century architects over the classical designs that Renaissance scholars had longingly harked back to.

RIGHT

The English rose is accompanied here in Pugin's wallpaper design for the Palace of Westminster by the crowned Portcullis emblem.

OPPOSITE AND DETAIL RIGHT

The door to the Queen of England's Robing Room in the Palace of Westminster, also created by Pugin, surpasses the intricacy and detail of his elaborate wallpaper and ceiling designs. It is a fine example of the Gothic Revival and a suitably grand doorway – fit for a queen.

ABOVE

Toddington Manor, Gloucestershire, England (1820). Built in 1820 by Lord Sudeley (1778–1858) with stylistic cues taken from the Houses of Parliament, the 300-room Toddington Manor, set in 124 acres of land, was acquired by artist Damien Hirst in 2005.

Chicago Tribune Tower, Chicago, USA (1923–25). By the early twentieth century, Gothic architectural style had evolved to such an extent that it signified not a representation of heaven on earth, but secular aspiration, ambition, success and quality.

Clad in Tuckahoe marble and with spires rising 100 metres from street level, St Patrick's Cathedral in New York is the largest decorated Gothic-Revival Catholic cathedral in North America.

One of the finest examples of Gothic Revival architecture in the US is St Patrick's Cathedral in New York, designed by James Renwick Jr (1818–1895). In uncanny parallel with his medieval forbears, Renwick Jr proved to be a prodigious talent at a very young age, entering Colombia University to study engineering at the age of 12, and graduating in 1836. Without formally studying architecture, Renwick gathered his understanding and appreciation of Gothic buildings from his travels throughout Europe, a fact that is clearly revealed in the mixture of French, German and English influences on the cathedral. Unlike the cathedrals that so influenced Renwick, the building of the current cathedral took a mere 21 years to complete, opening its doors in 1879.

Borrowing the now familiar architectural feature of soaring aspirational height, we can see an example of the Gothic cathedral's influence as late as 1922, in Chicago, Illinois. The Chicago Tribune Tower was built by the architects John Mead Howells (1868–1959) and Raymond Hood (1881–1934). The two architects met while studying in Paris, where they were clearly influenced by the original Gothic architecture so prevalent in the city. The proprietor of the *Chicago Tribune* was impressed by their proposal. Undoubtedly the complex arrangement of soaring ornamental masonry supported by buttresses, and its association with status, grandeur and success was not lost on him.

"The path to Paradise begins in Hell."

Dante Alighieri

ART

IN AN ERA when literacy was reserved for the ruling elite, the communication of ideas, instructions and information had to be either aural or visual. The large medieval church or cathedral was the ideal setting for controlling a willing and awestruck public – we know that their dramatic cavernous spaces and gravity defying architecture set the scene and atmosphere. But in support of this display of evangelizing power, there needed to be detail. It was all very well for the laity to sit and listen to the words of the liturgy, but in order to sear the doctrine in the memory there had to be visual stimulus, through allegory, symbolism and analogy. And that is where the artists came in.

As far as Western medieval thought was concerned, Jerusalem was literally at the geographical centre of the world, whereas – according to the popular belief – the extreme southern, eastern, and eventually northern edges of the known world were the exclusive location of barbaric heathen monsters. The early fifteenth-century compendium of travels known as the *Livre des Merveilles* (*c.*1410–12) accounted for the travels of explorers such as Marco Polo. No doubt eager to flex their imaginative skills, the painters interpreted Polo's description of "wild men" to include extraordinary physically deformed humanoids. The contemporaneous viewer had no reason to disbelieve what he or she saw, and we can safely assume that these images stoked the general populous' understanding of the barbaric, mysterious "other".

The simple, binary outlook that was understood by the masses and perpetuated by the church authority – good and evil, heaven and hell, Christian and heathen – were allegorical motifs that translated with intense visual clarity into medieval sculpture and painting. The medieval church's depictions of purgatory as a place to atone for one's lesser sins before being granted passage to the kingdom of heaven was both visceral and unambiguous. Sharing visual cues from Dante's *Divine Comedy* (1308–1321), the bas-relief sculpture on the façade of Orvieto Cathedral (1310–30) in Italy shows the tormented anguish of purgatory's inhabitants, with the horrors of hell just below them. If ever there was a guiding illustration warning against mortal sin and its consequences, then this is it.

ABOVE

Dance of Death *fresco at the Church of St Mary of the Rocks in Croatia. The dance of death as a reminder of mortality became a common image in medieval Europe. It was based on the thirteenth-century legend of three young hunters who one day confronted their own cadavers.*

Death was a phenomenon that occurred all too frequently and often without warning in fourteenth-century Europe, with the Black Death decimating huge swathes of people. Being prepared for death was therefore paramount. As a reminder of the indiscriminate power of death, the Croatian fresco by Vincent of Kastav, depicting the *Dance of Death* (1474), clearly illustrates people from all classes and of all types, interspersed with the skeletal vision of death. The flat, two-dimensional image, with the angular, jutting bones of the skeletons contrasting with the more curved and fluid human forms, has the curious effect of appearing animated, as though in a jerking awkward and discomforting dance. We can only imagine what the music must be like. Far more overt in its message is another fresco, *The Triumph of Death,* by an unknown artist, *c.*1450. In contrast to the Renaissance Gothic style that was prevalent on the Italian mainland, this Catalan work has scant redemptive or edifying qualities. It goes straight for the gory, macabre message that death always wins, and takes particular delight in taking the rich. Perhaps most macabre of all is the fact that this fresco – depicting the wild and violent figure of Death astride an equally horrifying horse – was painted for the chapel of a Sicilian hospital.

In a work that would not look out of place in the contemporary oeuvre of artists Jake and Dinos Chapman, Dieric Bouts' (1415–75) *Hell* (1470) from his *Last*

Judgment triptych is a nightmarish image of suffering and torture. We see half-human, half-beast demons, darkly scaled and taloned in stark contrast with the pale, naked vulnerability of the tormented humans. We even see one spiky-headed creature with a face in his chest, much like the easily as fantastical but (allegedly) earth-dwelling monsters from the *Livre des Merveilles.* Perhaps better known is Bouts' near contemporary, Hieronymous Bosch (1450–1516). While retaining the violence of Bouts' depictions, Bosch's work has the added element of mind-altering surrealism. As a precursor to the contemporary gothic tradition of splicing together strange and disturbing creatures from parts of even stranger ghouls and monsters, his work is second to none. Bosch's *Garden of Earthly Delights* (see pages 34–35) is an example of an imagination aflame with extraordinarily weird images. Such is the veracity with which Bosch fills the panels of his triptych that it seems almost as if he is trying to cleanse his mind of the characters inside. The Garden of Eden is depicted in the first panel with what appears to be an almost bored sense of obligation, so that he can get on with the increasingly weird and disturbing renditions in the following two panels.

Over two hundred years later, and drawing on his time as a young artist studying the old churches of London, William Blake (1757–1827) began his love affair and affinity with the Gothic aesthetic. Attracted to the Christian values

OPPOSITE

The Triumph of Death *(c.1450), Palermo, Italy. A straightforward and violent allegory of death, we see the clergy among the rich being trampled in the wake of the demonic horse, while the pious poor are spared.*

associated with the burgeoning Gothic Revival, the content of his work was not the high-impact visual onslaught of otherworldly violence and turmoil seen in the work of the likes of Bosch, but far more spiritual, atmospheric and measured. Blake understood that the way to create great art was through the clarity of line and the sublime grandeur of form – attributes he saw exemplified in the Gothic structures of the churches and cathedrals around him. His work, *God Creating Adam* (1795), would not look out of place adorning the stonework of a medieval church, with the compacted form so close to the picture plane as to look almost like a carving in shallow relief. Blake's powerful images and poetic works have ensured his longevity, latterly enjoying a contemporary revival through Thomas Harris' novel *Red Dragon* (1981) and the subsequent, darkly gripping film of the same name.

OPPOSITE
Hell *by Dieric Bouts the Elder, 1470. It's already too late for the poor souls depicted here. The composition of the painting is clearly structured downward, as the figures pile up, having literally reached rock bottom.*

LEFT
Housed in the Brooklyn Museum in New York, The Red Dragon and the Woman Clothed with the Sun *(1803–05) by William Blake is taken from a series of over 100 commissioned watercolours of the Bible, and depicts the Book of Revelation.*

The Gothic reverence of death, the afterlife and the display and adoration of relics – exemplified by the patrons of the medieval cathedrals – has also found a natural home in the secular world of contemporary art. One of the many contemporary artists who have appropriated the dramatic and death-centric elements of the gothic, via the ghoulish imaginings of nineteenth-century fiction, is Damien Hirst, who has updated some of the more well-known themes of death, the afterlife and the uncanny to accommodate the twenty-first century's obsessions and fears. It is no coincidence that an example of Gothic Revival architecture, Toddington Manor in Gloucestershire, England, has been bought by Hirst as an appropriate setting to house his vast collection of macabre art (see page 31). Famous for his animal carcasses in formaldehyde, powerful works that conjure images and narratives of purgatorial suspension, he also has a keen understanding of the power of symbolic association. One of the most iconic examples of this is Hirst's sculpture *For the Love of God* (2007). A human skull, after being cast in platinum, had its entire surface covered in 8601 flawless diamonds. The irrelevance of

(see page 31)

BELOW

Sarah Lucas,
Self Portrait with
Skull *(1997).*
The simplicity and
direct nature of
Lucas' work belies
a powerful sense of
dark and subversive
humour, often using
found objects to
create direct and
confrontational
objects.

material wealth when compared to the inevitability of death is made clear, yet there is a darkly comic element in the blatantly confrontational nature of the work, illustrating the futile defiance of those who try and buy longevity.

At a different end of the creative spectrum yet retaining the *memento mori* imagery of the skull in her work is Sarah Lucas, a contemporary of Damien Hirst. Her *Self Portrait with Skull* (1997) clearly took moments to create, and plainly the value of her skull does not match that of Hirst's creation. Yet despite these formal differences, the powerful symmetry between Lucas' defiant gaze and the dark hollows of the skull beneath, coupled with the symbolic birth-like placement between her legs of the grubby and disfigured skull are, in their simplicity and quotidian presentation, equally if not more potent.

OPPOSITE

Gabriel Orozco's Black Kites *(1997).*
Like his British contemporaries,
Orozco's use of the human skull is
both inventive and evocative. We can
imagine him contemplating mortality
as he handles the skull, attempting
to control or quantify death with a
checkerboard design painstakingly
inscribed with a graphite pencil.

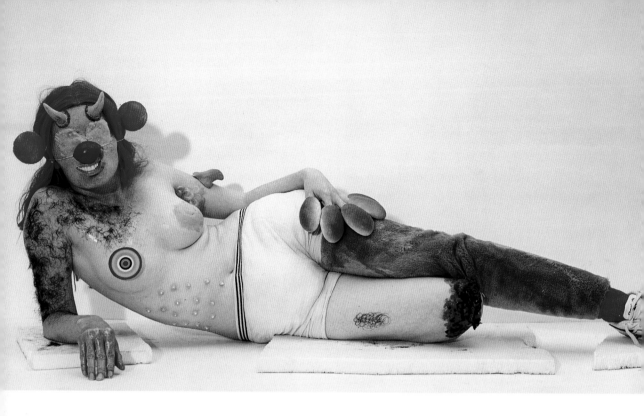

A telling attribute of the gothic theme in contemporary art is not only its propensity to use macabre or gory imagery, but in the viewer's willingness to participate; a desire to confront the darker side of humanity through a theatrical sense of self-imposed fear. In the safety of the gallery we can dare to go as close as possible, to scare ourselves, while at all times sharing a tacit agreement with the artist that as long as we're on the right side of the mortal coil, we're safe just to look. An artist that pushes this divide between life and death, reality and fiction, to its limits is the sculptor Ron Mueck. Mueck's sculpture, *Dead Dad* (1996–97) is extraordinary in its realism, so much so that when viewing it – despite our rational judgement – we instinctively respond to it as a real corpse. The fact that the sculpture's scale is half that of a real human does very little to convince us of its fiction; in fact, it has the effect of demanding even closer inspection. The viewer has to peer forward and get uncomfortably close. The human desire to create life from inanimate objects, with its related moral implication and suggestion of trampling on God's toes, is well-known and long lived – from the Pygmalion legend of the sculptor falling in love with his statue of Venus (only to have his prayers answered and the statue come to life), to the Jewish tradition of the Golem, Descartes' automaton Francine and of course Frankenstein's monster. Mueck continues this tradition of human verisimilitude. The fact that despite knowing the sculptures are made of silicone and fibreglass, we want to believe in them, to believe that as soon as our backs are turned they will open their eyes or exhale, proves that the tradition will continue to live on.

Other contemporary artists working with the human form, such as Olaf Breuning or David Almejd, deal firmly with the dark, nightmarish aspects of humanity. Olaf Breuning's *Sibylle* (1997) uses a culturally and art-historically recognizable pose, that of a reclining female looking directly (usually enticingly) at the viewer. Several binary themes associated with contemporary gothic culture are notably present in this photograph; the contrast between the familiarity and welcoming nature of the pose, and the repulsive mutilated detail, the violent splicing together of parts to try and create a whole, and the queasy forcing together of culturally symbolic objects – horns, a clown's nose, hot-dog buns. If Mueck's sculptures come close to the realization of the Pygmalion myth, Breuning's example shows what happens when it all goes wrong.

David Altmejd's work, *The Center* (2008) alludes to a state somewhere between the completion of the mad scientist's work and the unearthly spark of life that activates it. Altmejd captures the unknown liminal state between waking and sleeping, life and death. There is a serene power present in the work, the combination of closed eyes coupled with upright confident stance suggest that we are about to witness the monster's first breath, and its first view of the world. The theatrical narrative and content suggested by these works seize upon the contemporary cultural imagery that we have become so used to through film and literature, but also, more disconcertingly, they allude to the modern horror of mutilation and death that we as contemporary viewers are becoming increasingly anaesthetized to.

ABOVE

David Atmejd, The Center *(2008). The physiological and biological mechanisms that could potentially animate this figure are on the outside, while numerous disjointed hands appear to serve the body to some unknown end.*

Using real, known events as reference points in their work, brothers Jake and Dinos Chapman force together fact with horrific imagery, made all the more potent by our discomforting suspicion that the deeds depicted could have happened. *Hell* (1999–2000) is a nine-part diorama positioned in the shape of a swastika, using 5,000 tiny figurines, painstakingly hand-painted to depict Nazis or mutants engaged in acts of torture, mutilation and punishment. It seems that the scale of the objects are in diametrical opposition to the horrors that they depict; the smaller they are, the worse they behave. The details of the enacted scenes seem to come from the "what if…" school of creative thought more associated with a child's outlook (what if I put this doll's head on this animal's body…), an association which, when combined with the toy-like nature of the

figures, takes us somewhat unwillingly back to childhood and the ghouls and monsters of nightmares unchecked by adult rationale. One of the more powerful aspects of the work is the appeal to the voyeuristic intimacy that comes from viewing it. We cover our eyes and peep through our fingers, peering closely at the tiny figures. So long as we're on the outside looking in, we're safe, the glass of the vitrines acting like a border separating our reality from theirs. In the face of death, often meted out with horrific brutality, there is a dark and persistent humour. We are never sure whether the protagonists in the scenes created are so psychologically unhinged that they derive a cackling pleasure from their actions, or whether in fact, like us, sometimes the only way to deal with such brutality is through humour.

LEFT

Hell (detail, 1990–2000) by Jake and Dinos Chapman. Referencing the nightmarish conclusion of Nazi eugenics, within the brutal imagery there is a disturbing ambiguity concerning who (or what) is punishing whom, and whether such punishment can ever be justified.

The American artist Matthew Barney creates elaborate, full-scale films, bringing his fantastical narratives to stunning reality, blurring to the point of destruction any boundary between fact and fiction, dream and wakefulness. His five-film epic *Cremaster Cycle* (1994–2002), and subsequent exhibition of the same title, brings the nineteenth-century gothic themes of fabricated bodies, metaphoric objects, memory, fantasy, fear and the unknown firmly and elaborately into the twenty-first century. Barney not only splices together species and genders, but also subverts culturally accepted norms. The Dandy Satyr character depicted in *Cremaster 4,* and known as the Loughton Candidate, has either lost the horns usually associated with the hyper-masculine satyr or is waiting for them to develop, while the muscular torso and hairy beard we expect has been updated to a clean-shaven face in a dapper suit. These themes once again hark back to the lineage begun by the Pygmalion myth, but this time the author or creator of the hybrid is unknown. By now we are expected to simply believe in the existence of these contemporary satyrs and asexual humanoids. We have reached the point where we no longer question the motives behind their creation, nor the ethical consequence of their existence. Barney's combination of known and imagined objects, coupled with the high production value of his films, seamlessly cross the border from fiction into reality.

A common thread in the contemporary artistic examples given so far has been that of the inclusion, in some form or another, of the human form. A prevailing gothic theme, it allows the artist to explore the darker side of humanity and the afterlife through mutilation, gender re-imagining and muddling of species. Equally potent, however, is the use by contemporary artists of the theatrically staged installation, notable for its lack of humanoid figuration. Banks Violette's sculptural installations use the monochromatic palette we have come to associate with the contemporary gothic aesthetic, presenting objects laden with potent symbolism. In his work *Hate Them* (2004), he has tapped into a contemporary urban state of mind, creating something between an altar and something akin to a stage or drum set from a rock concert. His use of materials, combining slick reflective chrome and resin with dark, textured inverted cones have an arresting – and attractive – visual effect, alluding to the consumerist aesthetic of contemporary desirable objects sought out by a young, financially solvent generation. Despite the ambiguous nature of the dark shapes, the way they are displayed implies an invitation for the viewer to step up, take centre stage, and interact. Held out on what appear to be adjustable steel arms, the dark cones with flat, drum-like ends immediately suggest a mechanized intention, with an outcome that we can only guess at – our only assurance being that whatever happens, it's going to look, and sound, spectacular.

The implied presence of a figure or phantom, this time in the guise of memory, nightmare or fiction is an overwhelming theme in the series of *Cell* works, created by Louise Bourgeois (1911–2010) between 1986 and 1998.

OPPOSITE
Cremaster 5 *by Matthew Barney was shown at The Tate, London, in 1997. The artist himself appears as an actor in all but* Cremaster 1.

Using domestic objects to create hallucinatory figments, Bourgeois draws on her personal experiences growing up, and especially the overpowering role of her father. The objects are laden with metaphor and meaning, and the cage-like confines around the installations act as psychological boundaries between the time and space we exist in, and the timeless, unstable world beyond. They are also explicit reference to the artist's experiences of growing up as an ambitious young girl in France at the beginning of the twentieth century, keenly aware of the social, sexual and familial restraints around her. Bourgeois has inverted the gothic tradition of a misguided being playing God to conjure or create another, and instead turned the focus on herself as the object of creation, with all its concomitant flaws and psychoses. The *Cell* works are used as platforms or stages to depict scenes that arise from her state of being, and despite the strong personal aspect of the series, they engender an almost visceral empathy in those that view them. In the two installations *Red Room (Parents)* 1994 and *Red Room (Child)* 1994, we see a powerful depiction of the dystopian family. A comparison with Stanley Kubrick's *The Shining* (1980) comes readily to mind (see pages 112–13) – both works exploring familial destruction through madness and fear, as the wholesome conventions of father, mother and child are inverted or demonized. *Red Room (Parents)* presents an austere bedroom scene, with a symmetry and cleanliness contrasting with bizarre votive and symbolic objects evoking a latent violence. The blood-red sheets and pillowcases, echoed in the strange red globule hanging like a dark memory above, needs no explanation and provides a formal

link to the next *Cell, Red Room (Child).* In contrast to the
parent's room, this room contains a maddening asymmetry
of objects, wheels of thread appearing from the Bourgeois
family's tapestry restoration business like fragments of memory,
combining with dismembered body parts and the impotent
tools for escape – a ladder that's too short and too wide,
alongside a pair of forlorn suitcases. Traumatic experience
presented via memory and nightmare, the "other" is made real.
Through a seeming act of attempted catharsis, Bourgeois has
conjured into reality the darkest recess of her psyche, and in
turn, makes us uncomfortably aware of our own.

BELOW

Louise Bourgeois, Red Room
(Child), *1994. In contrast to
the finality of the parent's room,
this room is vibrant, unfinished
and erratic, suggesting possibility
and potential, and the struggle
against confinement.*

"The boundaries which divide Life from Death
are at best shadowy and vague. Who shall say
where the one ends, and where the other begins?"

Edgar Allan Poe

FICTION

STEPHEN KING has suggested that readers of H.P. Lovecraft, the early twentieth-century horror writer, may find that he becomes "a voice that whispers late at night, when sleep won't come and the moon peers coldly in the window. The voice whispering from inside the pillow." It's that kind of voice which has spoken for gothic fiction since the first weird tales of Horace Walpole (1717–97). "Attack the story like a radiant suicide," modern-day literary provocateur and Lovecraft fanatic Michel Houellebecq has advised writers, while eulogizing his idol. "Utter the great NO to life without weakness; then you will see a magnificent cathedral, and your senses, vectors of unutterable derangement, will map out an integral delirium that will be lost in the unnameable architecture of time." "Indispensable advice," King has concurred.

You can discern among those words of Houellebecq and King – highly contrasting writers themselves – the blend of poeticism, ghoulishness and romance that has come to define gothic fiction. If its origins are generally attributed to Walpole's *The Castle of Otranto*, subtitled on its second edition *A Gothic Story*, its virus has since spread far and wide, from high culture to potboiler trash. Mary Shelley's *Frankenstein*, Bram Stoker's *Dracula* and the works of Edgar Allan Poe are perhaps its signature totems, yet from Ann Radcliffe to Anne Rice, from the Brontës to Poppy Z. Brite, from Wilkie Collins to Colin Wilson, its "pleasing terrors" have scared and seduced. Today, with the books of J.K. Rowling and Stephenie Meyer labelled by some as gothic, it is bigger and badder – if often more bastardized – than ever. "Gothic" is a mercurial term. Perhaps it is entirely appropriate that gothic fiction began, melodramatically enough, in a murky cloud of deceit, confusion and subterfuge, with the author in question dismissed as a "trickster".

PREVIOUS PAGE

The Grim Reaper in Rackham's enigmatic illustration for the 1907 Eleanor Gates' novel, Good-Night.

BELOW

H.P. Lovecraft – "the horror writer's horror writer" – surrounded by the offspring of his psyche, as drawn by Dave Carson.

OPPOSITE

Edgar Allan Poe was the pioneering poet of gothic fiction. This illustration by Harry Clarke is from the 1923 edition of his Tales of Mystery and Imagination.

Not-so-humble Beginnings

Horace (Horatio) Walpole, the 4th Earl of Orford, wasn't your average wordsmith. A bona fide man of letters, the son of the first Prime Minister (Sir Robert Walpole) was also a Whig politician and an art historian. Arguably, *The Castle of Otranto* isn't even what he's most remembered for. That would be Strawberry Hill, the fanciful mansion he built in Twickenham, just outside London, wherein he revived elements of the Gothic architectural style long before its Victorian-era resurgence in popularity. It was he who coined the much-quoted epigram: "This world is a comedy to those that think, a tragedy to those that feel."

One presumes that Walpole was smiling to himself when he published *The Castle of Otranto* anonymously on Christmas Day, 1764, with a title page claiming it was translated from the original Naples-dialect Italian and that its long-lost text had been salvaged from a library. The book was glowingly received, so, within a few months, Walpole published his second edition, but this time admitting authorship, adding the subtitle *A Gothic Story* and elaborating on his motives: "The favourable manner in which this little piece has been received by the public, calls upon the author to explain the grounds on which he composed it: as an attempt to blend the two kinds of romance, the ancient and the modern. In the former all was imagination and improbability: in the latter, nature is always intended to be, and sometimes has been, copied with

BELOW

Strawberry Hill, the Twickenham mansion of Horace Walpole, author of The Castle of Otranto *and a multi-talented gothic "trickster".*

CASTLE OF OTRANTO. Ch. 3rd &c.
Theodore, conducting Isabella to the Cavern,
to protect her from the fury of Manfred.

success…" Some have seen Walpole's experiment of merging the two styles as a manifesto for gothic fiction.

Now, however, with the wizard behind the curtain revealed, a book that had just recently been hailed as a work of genius was denounced as fluffy and "preposterous". Its fascination with superstition and violence was apparently fine provided it came from a bygone age, but decidedly unacceptable in upper-class England. It contravened the progressive principles of the Enlightenment. Almost accidentally, Walpole had committed an act of destabilizing subversion, with the first gothic novel defying easy categorization and noisily rattling set notions of culture.

With its fusion of supernatural prophecies and believable individual characters, *The Castle of Otranto* begins with a bang. Manfred, lord of the castle, and his family prepare for the wedding of his ailing son Conrad and the princess Isabella. But just before the wedding is to commence, Conrad is killed by a giant helmet that falls out of the sky and lands on him. Now that's an opening! Fantastical situations persist; realistic people react to them. Other traits patented here, which became staples of the gothic novel genre, include a cursed or tainted family, a fearsome mystery, hidden passages and creaky doors opening without anyone knowingly opening them, eerie noises and a damsel in distress, prone to fainting, fleeing from an ill-intentioned male. The ending is, of course, sorrowful.

ABOVE LEFT
A 1794 illustration from Walpole's The Castle of Otranto, *the first gothic novel.*

ABOVE RIGHT
A 1765 engraving from The Castle of Otranto, *in which knights and damsels in distress set the gothic tone.*

From Terror to Horror

Walpole was once described somewhat unkindly by an enemy as "a hermaphrodite horse". On the other hand, Ann Radcliffe (1764–1823), born Ann Ward in Holborn, London, in the same year that Walpole's landmark book emerged, was "said to be exquisitely proportioned… beautiful… especially her eyes, eyebrows and mouth". Something of a recluse, albeit married to an editor, little is known of her life off the page; Christina Rossetti began writing a biography of her but gave up because there was insufficient information. Her novels certainly made money, yet one obituary read: "She never appeared in public, nor mingled in private society, but kept herself apart, like the sweet bird that sings its solitary notes, shrouded and unseen."

Radcliffe's work saw the critic Nathan Drake refer to her as "the Shakespeare of romance", and she did quote the Bard frequently. She penned long, vivid descriptions of travel and landscapes, but her tales would also suggest and allude to the supernatural. The twist was that, finally, she would offer a rational explanation for events, which was "explained Gothicism". The explanation of the weird phenomena – everything is all right really, folks – granted her six novels, which championed the rights of women and respectability. Morals and reason win the day.

Across the 1780s and 1790s, she published *The Castles of Athlin and Dunbayne, A Sicilian Romance* (in two volumes), *The Romance of the Forest*

RIGHT
Ann Radcliffe's gothic classic The Mysteries of Udolpho *was later parodied by Jane Austen in* Northanger Abbey. *This illustration from 1794 is by Mary Byfield.*

and *The Mysteries of Udolpho* – the last was the gothic classic parodied by Jane Austen in *Northanger Abbey*. Radcliffe herself began to have doubts about where the genre was heading, and *The Italian* (1797) was a reaction to *The Monk* by Matthew G. Lewis (1775–1818).

After her death, her husband published her unfinished essay "On the Supernatural in Poetry", which emphasized the difference between her aim of promoting the sensation of "terror" and Lewis's of going for out-and-out "horror". *The Mysteries of Udolpho* (1794) remains the archetypal work of gothic fiction, in which put-upon heroine Emily (virtuous, sensitive, artistic) suffers the death of her father, fright nights in a shadowy castle, which one Dracula might have inhabited, and much brooding villainy. Radcliffe was a vast influence on diverse exponents of all wings of the genre, from Sir Walter Scott, who called her "the founder", to Poe, to the Marquis de Sade, who observed that gothic novels were a consequence of "revolutionary shocks felt throughout the whole of Europe". And if you wanted your gothic fiction shocking, *The Monk* raised the ante. Its publication in 1796 caused an explosion of debate and controversy. Lewis knowingly lampooned Radcliffe, making explicit the violence and unseemliness that was subtly implied in her work. *The Monk*, which included bleeding nuns and scenes of rape of a virtuous woman by her brother – a monk – was denounced as obscene and blasphemous, even by poet Samuel Taylor Coleridge. Yet it opened another dark passageway, which, as Radcliffe pointed out, was more "horror" than "terror". As would happen in gothic cinema, a fissure opened between the gruesomely graphic and the stylishly aesthetic. If the school of Radcliffe were *Vertigo* and *The Innocents*, Lewis's followers were *Saw* and *Hostel*.

The next wave of gothic fiction in the Romantic era reverted to a degree of restraint, flourishing through the poetry of Coleridge, Wordsworth and Shelley, which was gothic in that it strove for what Wordsworth called an "overflow of powerful feeling". Swooned Shelley, "The pleasure that is in sorrow is sweeter than the pleasure of pleasure itself." Coleridge's *The Rime of the Ancient Mariner* and *Christabel* were influenced by the German "Schauerroman" (shudder novel). Keats' *The Lamia* and Byron's *The Giaour* evoked both shudders and a sense of the sublime. Their verses played off the fiction of the day. And it was Byron

OPPOSITE

Keats' The Lamia – later the source of a Peter Gabriel lyric for Genesis – involved snakes mutating into attractive women. Illustration by Herbert James Draper, c.1909.

I heard, and in my soul discerned
Two voices in the air.

LEFT

"Water, water everywhere…" Coleridge's The Rime of the Ancient Mariner *saw Romantic poetry go gothic.*

who nudged Mary Shelley to write the book that moved us from Romantic-era gothic to full-blown Victorian gothic. Now, the human (or not) body itself tended to replace the castle as the site of the uncanny events.

Mary Shelley (1797–1851) was the daughter of political philosopher William Godwin (his gothically inclined novel *Caleb Williams*, concerning a psychological breakdown, was an influence on her writing) and feminist writer Mary Wollstonecraft. Mary Shelley authored stories, novels, plays, essays, biographies and travel pieces, as well as editing the work of her husband Percy Bysshe Shelley, but will always be best remembered for the book she wrote aged just 18 (and published, at first anonymously, two years later): *Frankenstein, The Modern Prometheus* (1818).

It was a dark and stormy night… except it wasn't. It was an idyllic summer in 1816 near Geneva, when Byron challenged the holidaying group (himself, John Polidori, Claire Clairmont and the Shelleys, not yet married) to write a ghost or horror story. Mary wrote hers based on a dream she'd had, in which a scientist created "new" life, only to be horrified by what he'd done. (Percy did help in the writing, and Mary, while denying it was a collaboration, graciously acknowledged that "but for his incitement, it would never have taken the form in which it was presented to the world".)

Frankenstein is conventionally gothic in its fusion of startling and visceral story with imaginative, provocative themes. Yet its focus willfully strays from the plot to zoom in on the anguish of scientist Victor Frankenstein (the creator of the grotesque creature, rebelling against nature) and the perils of his narcissistic ambition. In some ways, it is also the first science fiction story. It has Biblical parallels, too: the creature – also referred to in the book as "monster", "wretch", "fiend", "daemon", "being", "vile insect" and merely "It" – calls himself, when talking to the doctor, "the Adam of your labours". Elsewhere, he sighs that he is not the desired Adam but "your fallen angel". In Greek mythology, at the behest of Zeus, Prometheus created mankind in the image of the gods, but was subsequently punished – chained to a rock for eternity – when he stole fire from Zeus. (Percy Shelley wrote his own *Prometheus Unbound* in 1820.)

The initial response to *Frankenstein* was lukewarm. "A tissue of horrible and disgusting absurdity," claimed the *Quarterly Review*. Sir Walter Scott used the word "genius" but *The British Critic* boorishly boomed, "The writer of it is, we understand, a female: this is an aggravation of that which is the prevailing fault of the novel." In our more enlightened age, in which *Frankenstein* seems a visionary premonition of scientific progress, Stephen King has acclaimed the much-filmed tale's durable influence, citing it as a Shakespearean tragedy, yet qualified his praise with: "Its classical unity is broken only by the author's uncertainty as to where the fatal flaw lies – is it in Victor's hubris (usurping a power that belongs only to God), or in his failure to take responsibility for his creation after endowing it with the life-spark?" Perhaps, within that nebulous gap of uncertainty, much of gothic fiction since has danced.

LEFT
Frontispiece image from the first edition of Frankenstein. *"I saw the dull yellow eye of the creature opened; it breathed hard and a convulsive motion agitated its limbs…"*

Victorian Gothic

With the chains on gothic fiction broken by Frankenstein's creature, the nineteenth century now saw the glory age of Victorian gothic. Although it was being panned by critics, its tropes by this time so familiar that Jane Austen could parody them, its key writers found new dark corridors to explore. Walter Scott was publishing *Letters on Demonology and Witchcraft* (1885), and by 1837 Nathaniel Hawthorne was representing America with *Twice-Told Tales*. French poet Théophile Gautier's 1836 short story *La Morte Amoureuse* told of a priest who falls for a beauty, who, as it turns out, is a vampire. And now the generation of giants enters the gothic stage, with subsequent decades marking the heyday of Edgar Allan Poe, Charles Dickens, Wilkie Collins and the Brontë sisters.

While nobody would confidently term *Wuthering Heights* by Emily Brontë or *Jane Eyre* by Charlotte Brontë as "horror", the two books – both published in 1847, the same year as the more obviously scary, if less highbrow, "penny dreadful" *Varney the Vampire or The Feast of Blood* by James Malcolm Rymer, which popularized vampire fiction – contain darker, starker elements that ensure their place in the gothic canon. *Wuthering Heights* was Emily's only novel, centring on the destructive, jealous infatuation amid the wild and windy Yorkshire Moors of Cathy and Heathcliff, and was considered brutal by its era. "'Wuthering Heights' is the name of Mr Heathcliff's dwelling. 'Wuthering' being a significant provincial adjective, descriptive of the atmospheric tumult to which its station is exposed in stormy

ABOVE

Walter Scott's Letters on Demonology and Witchcraft *showed how seriously gothic was taken.*

RIGHT

Théophile Gautier's La Morte Amoureuse *told of a priest lured by a beautiful vampire.*

COMPOSITIONS DE A.-P. LAURENS

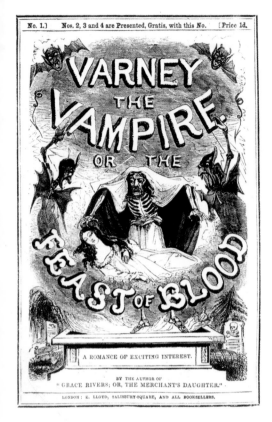

VARNEY THE VAMPIRE. OR THE FEAST OF BLOOD

A ROMANCE OF EXCITING INTEREST.

BY THE AUTHOR OF
" GRACE RIVERS; OR, THE MERCHANT'S DAUGHTER."

LONDON: E. LLOYD, SALISBURY-SQUARE, AND ALL BOOKSELLERS.

VARNEY THE VAMPYRE; OR, THE FEAST OF BLOOD.   153

FLORA ENCOUNTERS VARNEY IN THE SUMMER-HOUSE.

weather." Dante Gabriel Rossetti called it a "fiend of a book, an incredible monster". Cathy's entanglement in ghostly apparitions – and Heathcliff's demonic side – conform to gothic dynamics.

Charlotte's equally intense *Jane Eyre* also sees a growing young woman, a proto-feminist, fall under the spell of the Byronic and troubled Mr Rochester, who has dark secrets to spare, in a gothic manor where strange noises and events are not always instantly explicable. The supernatural is hinted at in Jane's dreams, her keen feeling for ghosts and the lightning that strikes the chestnut tree on the night she agrees to marry Rochester. Deemed "anti-Christian" by some at the time, *Jane Eyre* was, in fact, a protest at Victorian repression and an act of class war, ahead of its time. "Conventionality is not morality," Brontë wrote in her preface to the second edition. "Self-righteousness is not religion… appearance should not be mistaken for truth."

Just prior to these two literary landmarks, two authors often tagged as the godfathers of gothic rose to prominence. Poe, the high priest of cerebral chills, was, of course, one. Charles Dickens (1812–70) may not be taught in schools as gothic, but a serious look across his esteemed career shows that every element of the genre is present and purposeful in *Oliver Twist*, *The Old Curiosity Shop*, *Our Mutual Friend* and – most overtly – the unfinished *The Mystery of Edwin Drood* (1870). Dickens had devoured gothic novels as a teenager and put his own

ABOVE LEFT
The cover of Varney the Vampire *by James Malcolm Rymer. Although the book was deemed a "penny dreadful" when published in 1847, it proved hugely popular.*

ABOVE RIGHT
This image taken from inside Varney the Vampire *shows Flora's terror at encountering Varney in the summerhouse.*

ABOVE

*Edgar Allan Poe
believed that terror
was "of the soul".
He died in 1849
when aged just 40.*

RIGHT

*Arthur Rackham's
striking visual
interpretation of
Poe's* A Descent Into
the Maelstrom.

spin on their melodramatic atmosphere, usually within a more modern, urban frame. *Bleak House* – a festival of fog – and *Great Expectations* also played on the contrast between the order and comfort of affluence and the chaos and struggle of poverty. His last novel, *Edwin Drood*, is explicit in its investigations of murder, though, due to Dickens' death, its mystery remains forever unsolved.

The innovations of Edgar Allan Poe (1809–49) changed gothic fiction forever. Poe delved headlong into the psychological aspects of his characters, as they – more often than not – slid into insanity. Criticized as "too German", he riposted that "terror is not of Germany, but of the soul". While his 1839 classic *The Fall of the House of Usher* does revel in set-pieces of loopy aristocrats and madness, it reaches its claws inside the reader's psyche. Across such seminal works as *Tales of the Grotesque and Arabesque, The Pit and the Pendulum, The Masque of the Red Death, A Descent into the Maelstrom, The Black Cat* and *The Cask of Amontillado,* Poe dealt with, well, death mostly. At first, he wrote detective stories; Sir Arthur Conan Doyle even said, "Where was the detective fiction story until Poe breathed the breath of life into it?"

Poe initially dabbled with gothic fiction just as satire, to appeal to the public, but his mind had a penchant for overrunning the runway. Variously denounced as "vulgar" or "too poetical", even Poe's *New York Tribune* obituary (hijacked by an editor with a grudge) was unsettling: "Edgar Allan Poe is dead. He died (at 40) in Baltimore the day before yesterday. This announcement will

startle many, but few will be grieved by it." Poe was painted as a depraved, drink-and-drugs maniac. He wasn't, although he had taken to drink after the illness, then death, of his wife Virginia. His recurring theme of a beautiful woman dying is the one thing in his work that's straightforward to explain.

With many of his lines now crucial to the genre's moods and rhythms, Poe remains the true poet of gothic fiction. One could not catch the essence of it more accurately – yet, somehow, evasively – than Poe: "All that we see or seem is but a dream within a dream." "We loved with a love that was more than love." "The boundaries which divide Life from Death are at best shadowy and vague. Who shall say where the one ends, and where the other begins?" "Science has not yet taught us if madness is or is not the sublimity of the intelligence." Such phrases define and deify the gothic.

Detectives and Demons

If Poe were a pioneer of both gothic fiction and detective stories, T.S. Eliot claimed that the latter genre was "invented by Collins and not by Poe". Wilkie Collins (1824–89), mentored by Dickens, influenced crime writers for generations to come, and his novel *The Moonstone* (1868) patented some staples: the English country house, a broad cast of potential suspects, an idiosyncratic sleuth who solves things brilliantly in a way the police couldn't. Yet it's arguably *The Woman in White,* published nine years earlier, for which Collins is best remembered. Indeed, his own chosen epitaph (at Kensal Green Cemetery, London) was "Author of *The Woman in White* and other works". The title hints at how gothic it is: a young art teacher encounters a distressed, mystery woman, escaped from an asylum, then falls in love with her lookalike. There are identity switches, typhoid fever, delusions and secrets. As the poet Swinburne observed: "What brought good Wilkie's night perdition? / Some demon whispered – Wilkie! Have a mission!"

Demons also whispered to the French poet Charles Baudelaire, whose *Les Fleurs du Mal* (1857) was a breakthrough work in gothic poetry, and to American satirist-journalist Ambrose Bierce – nicknamed "Bitter Bierce" – whose motto was "nothing matters", and who authored ghost stories and *The Devil's Dictionary*. Those demons were frenetically busy, as the morbidly obsessed-with-mortality *fin de siècle* brought another rush of gothic masterpieces.

Son of a Welsh vicar, Arthur Machen (1863–1947) was a devotee of the mystical and the occult and an author of supernatural and fantasy fiction. Stephen King has called his 1894 novella *The Great God Pan* "maybe the best horror story in the English language". It caused a scandal for its sexual and violent content – which boosted sales. Machen's later writings were less overtly "decadent", though he argued that his writing sought a form of transcendence, lifting the lid on the everyday and humdrum to reveal the madness (and sex and death) simmering just below. His avowed aim was a literature of "ecstasy", which he defined as consisting of "rapture, beauty, adoration, wonder, awe, mystery… desire for the unknown". Lovecraft was a fan, writing, "There is in Machen an ecstasy of fear that all other living men are too obtuse or timid to capture, and that even Poe failed to envisage in all its starkest abnormality."

Gothic Giants

Robert Louis Stevenson (1850–94) was a popular star of the era, but his reputation faded later as he was bracketed as "just" a successful writer of children's and horror stories. That reputation has since swung back to favour, but the *Treasure Island* author has always stood firm as a giant of the gothic, thanks to *The Body-Snatcher* (1884) and, chiefly, *The Strange Case of Dr Jekyll and Mr Hyde* (1886). This fable of a good-evil split personality has lent its name to a syndrome that's still (over)used in cinema as well as fiction. Stevenson was sick with a fever in bed when he wrote the first draft in three days, yelling at his wife when she woke him from what she'd assumed was a nightmare: "I was dreaming a fine bogey tale!" The battling impulses of heaven and hell within one man, the

civilized versus the animal, the duel between "outward respectability and inward lust" represent a dialogue very Victorian and very, very gothic.

Oscar Wilde's only published novel, *The Picture of Dorian Gray* (1890), was met with outrage, many advocating prosecution on moral grounds. With its famed Faustian theme of a young man whose unfading beauty is paid for with his

soul (a painting of him shows the ravages of indulgence, instead of his face), this now-respected classic of world literature, influenced by Joris-Karl Huysmans' *A Rebours (Against Nature),* was slammed as "contaminating", "unclean" and likely to "taint every young mind that comes into contact with it". Wilde's preface argued, "There is no such thing as a moral or an immoral book. Books are well written, or badly written. That is all. The nineteenth-century dislike of realism is the rage of Caliban seeing his own face in a glass."

Almost as controversial were H.G. Wells' *The Island of Dr Moreau* (1896), where a Frankenstein-like scientist creates human-like beings from animals through vivisection, and which Wells called "an exercise in youthful blasphemy", and Henry James' ghost-story novella *The Turn of the Screw* (1898). Riddled with a most enigmatic evil, this became the inspiration for the 1961 gothic cinema pinnacle *The Innocents.*

RIGHT
Bram Stoker's
Dracula – *wood
engraving shown –
was a landmark in
gothic fiction.*

Dracula Rises

Sandwiched between the years of publication of these last two works came another of the true titans of terror, Bram Stoker's *Dracula*. "I did not sleep well," writes Stoker during its opening chapter, "though my bed was comfortable enough, for I had all sorts of queer dreams." Count Dracula has fuelled the darker dreams of many generations since, and is now – thanks to his apparently endless cinematic charisma – one of the most adapted and reinvented icons of popular culture. Coming up with the tale of the vampiric Count, who yearns to relocate from Transylvania to England and is thwarted by Professor Van Helsing and his team, Irish-born Stoker defined the mythology of vampires the way we know it today: laced with sex and oddly alluring to women. In its day, the book was received as just a good adventure yarn, and it didn't sell well until Stoker's widow smartly re-promoted it on the back of the *Nosferatu* films of the 1920s and 1930s. It's never been out of print since, and it seems almost every week a new dashing young actor reinterprets the role on the big or small screen. In 1987, the *Daily Mail* hailed it as THE classic of gothic horror, adding, "In seeking a parallel to this weird, powerful and horrorful story, our mind reverts to such tales as *The Mysteries of Udolpho*, *Frankenstein* and *The Fall of the House of Usher* – but Dracula is even more appalling in its gloomy fascination than any one of these."

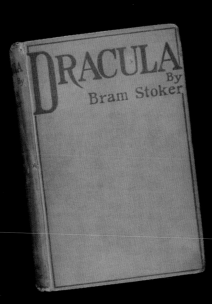

LEFT
The first edition of Stoker's classic tale, 1897.

Recent Interpretations

OPPOSITE

The American pulp magazine Weird Tales – *this issue dates from the mid-1930s – published the writing of H.P. Lovecraft, among others.*

And so the gothic strode into the twentieth century, established now as a genre that had overcome ridicule and brooked no resistance. In England, M.R. James and Hugh Walpole were among the frontrunners, with the scholarly James' ghost stories abandoning tired traditions: in his words, "the ghost should be malevolent or odious".

Sir Arthur Conan Doyle may be best known for creating Sherlock Holmes – still Dracula's main rival as a popular crossover star – but the prolific Scot, a fan of Stoker and a friend of Houdini, emitted plenty of (even) murkier characters, not least those reprinted in his stories in American pulp magazines like *Weird Tales*. Walter de la Mare's short story collections *The Riddle* (1923) and *The Connoisseur* (1926) offered significant ghost or supernatural tales. Daphne du Maurier's 1938 novel *Rebecca*, influenced by *Jane Eyre*, was filmed by Hitchcock, as was her short story *The Birds*, published in 1952. Her short story *Don't Look Now* became a classily unnerving 1973 Nicolas Roeg film. Du Maurier deplored her reputation as a "romantic" novelist, pointing out her frequent use of the paranormal and sinister, and aligning herself with the reputation of Wilkie Collins.

The gaunt, pale Howard Phillips Lovecraft (1890–1937) became the new horror writer's horror writer. Little known during his lifetime, he is now revered. (His novel *The Case of Charles Dexter Ward*, involving the resurrection of human remains, was published posthumously in 1941.) Frequently ill as a child in Providence, Rhode Island (where that book is set), he suffered night terrors; it's easy to see where his muse quivered. His work was dismissed as pulp, but later rehabilitated, though even then the eminent critic Edmund Wilson proclaimed sniffily, "the only real horror in most of these fictions is the horror of bad taste and bad art". Yet Joyce Carol Oates noted his "incalculable influence on succeeding generations", and more recently, as we've seen, he has been hailed as the greatest by everyone from King to Houellebecq.

Lovecraft's matchlessly dark view of the world involves a stormy brew of science, atheism, mythology, guilt, paranoia and contempt for humanity. His work has generally been placed into three categories: his "macabre" stories (1905–20), his "dream cycle" stories (1920–7) and the fictional cosmos of the "Cthulhu Mythos" stories, the imaginative leaps of which have influenced current-day stars such as Neil Gaiman and Alan Moore. Misanthrope extraordinaire Houellebecq admiringly sums up Lovecraft's "attitude" as an "absolute hatred of the world in general, aggravated by an aversion to the modern world in particular". "Sometimes," pondered Lovecraft, "I believe that this less material life is our truer life, and that our vain presence on the terraqueous globe is itself secondary."

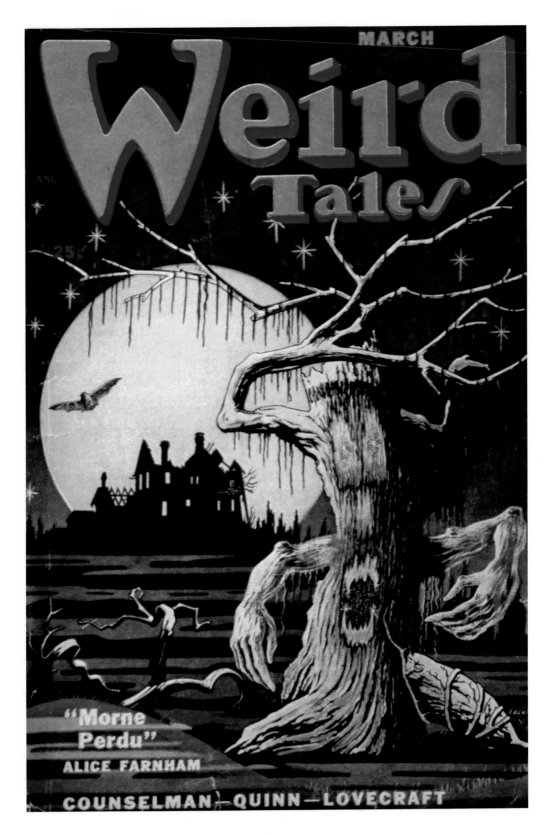

MARCH

Weird Tales

25¢

"Morne Perdu"
ALICE FARNHAM

COUNSELMAN—QUINN—LOVECRAFT

American Gothic

American Gothic was empowered by Lovecraft's fearlessness, and by the 1950s novels like Richard Matheson's zombie landmark *I Am Legend* and Robert Bloch's *Psycho* (also a Hitchcock film). "The man next door may be a monster," said Bloch, who had been mentored by Lovecraft. It was Bloch who came up with the quip, later borrowed by King: "Despite my ghoulish reputation, I really have the heart of a small boy. I keep it in a jar on my desk."

The sub-genre Southern Gothic brought the macabre to – or from – the American South, often focusing on disturbed individuals who meddle in hoodoo or voodoo, all depicted against decaying and once-aristocratic backdrops. Social issues were explored: this wasn't just about cheap chills, though magic realism was utilized. Nobel

ABOVE

Richard Matheson's
I Am Legend
*familiarized readers
with the fearsome
zombie, who has
never looked back.*

RIGHT

Robert Bloch's
Psycho *gave
Alfred Hitchcock
some compellingly
creepy ideas.*

Nobel Prize-winner William Faulkner was one of the chief exponents of Southern Gothic in his books from the 1930s like *Sanctuary, Light in August* and *Absalom, Absalom!* Other esteemed literary figures such as Truman Capote, Harper Lee, Tennessee Williams and Flannery O'Connor were intermittently associated with the movement. Latterly, Harry Crews was called "the Hieronymus Bosch of Southern Gothic".

The Feast of All Saints and *The Witching Hour* by New Orleans-born Anne Rice also come under that mantle, though her key contributions to gothic fiction are three books of *The Vampire Chronicles: Interview with the Vampire* (1976), *The Vampire Lestat* (1985) and *The Queen of the Damned* (1988). Rice's books have sold close to 100 million copies, placing her among gothic's all-time popular greats. The central antihero of Lestat de Lioncourt, a French nobleman turned into a vampire in the eighteenth century (played by Tom Cruise in Neil Jordan's 1994 adaptation) has proven irresistible to film-makers. Rice, interestingly, renounced her Christianity in 2010, stating that she remained "committed" to Christ but did not want to belong to a "quarrelsome, hostile, deservedly infamous group".

The British Approach

Gothic fiction in Britain, in the second half of the twentieth century, ranged in tone and timbre from Mervyn Peake's *Gormenghast* trilogy (1946–59) – with the brooding presence of Gormenghast Castle looming over all – to Angela Carter's unique spins on feminism and fairy-tales in works such as *The Magic Toyshop* (1967) and *The Bloody Chamber* (1979). J.G. Ballard took science fiction into post-apocalyptic realms (*The Drowned World*) and erotica past taboos (*Crash*), but his most gothic offering was *The Atrocity Exhibition* (1970), the title of which was lifted by Joy Division on their album *Closer*. A set of highly provocative short stories (or "condensed novels"), it depicts the mind of the individual being invaded and ravaged by modern mass media: the new, threatening, outwardly appealing, monster of our age. A near-contemporary of Ballard, Colin Wilson, whose death in December 2013 went criminally overlooked by the literary establishment, was a prolific philosopher and novelist who wrote of existentialism, the occult and the paranormal with vision and fluidity. His best book remains the 1956 non-fiction hit *The Outsider,* but his studies of murder and crime also cut to the bone. The sci-fi horror of *The Mind Parasites* (1967) was based on Lovecraft's "Cthulhu Mythos" tales, after August Derleth – Lovecraft's first publisher – protested that Wilson had called Lovecraft "sick".

OPPOSITE
Mervyn Peake scans sketches. His Gormenghast *trilogy captivated a generation.*

LEFT
The second book saw the young Titus Groan yearning to rebel against ritual.

ABOVE
British author Colin Wilson's now under-rated The Outsider *(1956) discussed social alienation and popularized existentialism in his home country.*

Entering the Mainstream

Today, the "outsiders" and the "sick" seem more mainstream and in ruder health than at almost any previous time. Stephen King has sold more than 350 million books, and it sometimes feels that the same number of them have been filmed. Since the 1970s horror boom, King has given us stand-outs like *The Shining, Pet Sematary, Carrie* and *Salem's Lot* (once described as *Peyton Place* meets *Dracula*). Riding along with his first wave then were James Herbert (*The Rats, The Fog*) and Clive Barker (*Weaveworld*). Dean Koontz (*Demon Seed*) and Poppy Z. Brite (*Lost Souls*) have popularly re-booted the genre. Among the many books of the Pulitzer-nominated Joyce Carol Oates, *Bellefleur, Zombie* and *First Love: A Gothic Tale* are just three with the G-word making its presence felt.

Few books of recent decades have caused as much of a love-hate ruckus as Bret Easton Ellis' transgressive postmodern shocker *American Psycho* (1991), told in the first person by serial killer Patrick Bateman. He's a cold monster created by consumer culture. A rage-magnet for the self-proclaimed moral majority upon publication, *American Psycho* was, two decades later, adapted as a West End musical.

RIGHT

Joyce Carol Oates – Gothic AND Pulitzer-nominated. Bellefleur *was the first in her "Gothic Saga" and involved prophecies and family curses.*

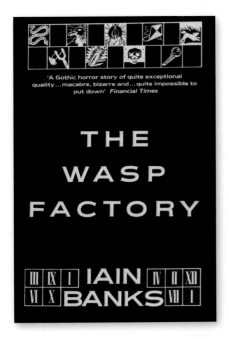

Susan Hill's 1983 novel *The Woman in Black* was recently made into a highly successful Hammer film, while the sad death of Iain Banks drew many eulogies for his 1984 masterpiece-of-weird *The Wasp Factory*. Neil Gaiman's award-winning graphic novels and short fiction continue to increase in popularity, while authors like Sarah Waters and the two-time Man Booker prizewinner Hilary Mantel happily stir uncompromising elements of Gothicism into their acclaimed, multi-faceted books. Many embraced the gothic glimpses within J.K. Rowling's all-conquering *Harry Potter* series, while Stephenie Meyer's *Twilight* franchise gave a hungry young generation an attack of the vapours with a boy-band version of vampires. The films fed the popularity of the fantasy-romance books as teenage Bella – a "danger magnet" – and 104-year-old Edward swooned over each other.

As gothic fiction grows and grows, let us recall with ambivalence Lucy Westenra's diary in Chapter 11 of *Dracula*, and her premature sighs of relief: "Somehow, I do not dread being alone tonight, and I can go to sleep without fear. I shall not mind any flapping outside the window. Oh, the terrible struggle that I have had against sleep so often of late… with such unknown horrors as it has for me. How blessed are some people whose lives have no fears, no dreads… I never liked garlic before, but tonight it is delightful! There is peace in its smell. I feel sleep coming already. Goodnight, everybody." Yet is there a voice whispering inside her pillow? Inside yours?

"It is a perfect night for mystery and horror.
The air itself is filled with monsters."

FILM

PREVIOUS PAGE
*F.W. Murnau's
Faust (1926) was
the most expensive
and elaborate
film ever made by
German film studio
UFA until Fritz
Lang's Metropolis
the following year.*

BELOW
*Tod Browning's
Dracula introduced
Bela Lugosi to the
cinema-going public
in 1931.*

GOTHIC FILM, which cast a sinister shadow in the brightly lit temples of early cinema, has grown in presence ever since. Appropriating the subversive shudders of gothic literature, it has for a century infiltrated popular culture, increasingly taking centre stage. Labelled "the dark heart of film" by the British Film Institute (BFI), it has come – quite literally – to haunt us, through decades of murky mythology.

Vampires, werewolves, ghosts and monsters are now a well-recognized visual vocabulary. Count Dracula and Frankenstein's creation have evolved from tuppenny carnival freaks into complex characters, riddled with subtexts and symbolism, suitable for extensive televisual probing. The living dead are a storytelling staple. Ghosts are a given, sometimes comforting, plot device. Vampires in general have finessed their way from hideous ghouls to sensuous heart-throbs, and Dracula is thought to be neck and neck (if you will) with Sherlock Holmes as the most frequently portrayed personage in movie history.

Gothic cinema isn't just about scares or frights and "terror" or "horror". It's about a sense of mystery, fairy stories for grown-ups, and old dark houses with novel secrets. It can be about romance, passion, eternal love: for (almost)

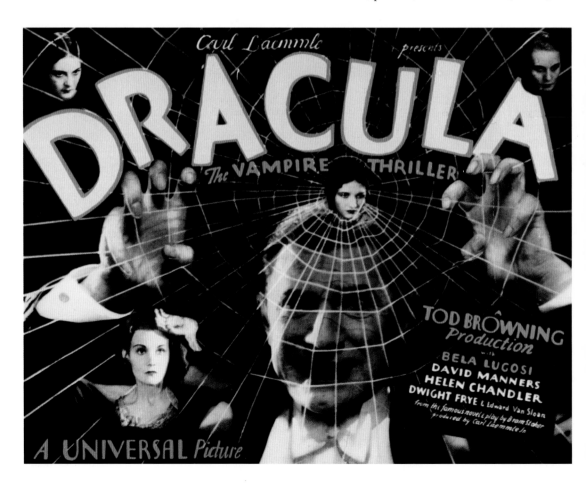

LEFT
Nosferatu *(1922),*
directed by F.W.
Murnau, gave
birth to vampire
movies and remains
the greatest silent
"horror" film of all
time. The hideous
vampire was played
by Max Schreck.

every beast, a beauty. And it has been richly represented in different ways at different times across the planet. From British Folk Gothic to American Southern Gothic, from Japan to Italy, from *Nosferatu* and *Vampyr* in the 1920s and 1930s to *Black Swan* and *Berberian Sound Studio* in the 2010s, it has blossomed, or shivered, into its own peculiar art form. It reflects our primal fears and hidden desires, drawing on the language of dreams and waking nightmares, serving as catharsis and catalyst: compelling, disturbing, deathlessly popular and, at its best, powerfully poetic. Classics as diverse as *Sunset Boulevard* (1950) and *Blade Runner* (1982) have been championed as gothic. If these films unnerve us, it is because we have chosen to be unnerved, willing victims of psychological meddling and implicit or explicit menace.

     Some might say that gothic cinema caters mainly to teenagers, prone to embrace extreme emotion and melodrama. Fans would counter that the genre bravely faces issues such as death, mortality, insecurity, guilt, moral duty and loneliness head-on. If the low-end shocks are sometimes tacky, the superior gothic work reaches hallucinatory aesthetic heights. It brings to the surface of our consciousness elements of dread and foreboding, which we conventionally suppress on a daily basis as we exist in denial. If you decide to walk around on an average day moaning that we're all going to die, society will certainly view you as a weirdo. In the world of gothic cinema, such revelations are mere entry-level musings. There is breathy, whispered intimacy to these films, wherein the average day is both elevated and debased, through strange yet curiously plausible interventions. And anyway, as Klaus Kinski's Dracula sighs in Werner Herzog's

1979 gothic great *Nosferatu the Vampyre*, "Death is not the worst. There are things more horrible than death."

A century ago, the first wave of gothic classics emerged from German expressionism. Robert Wiene's *The Cabinet of Dr. Caligari* arrived in 1919, and the following year saw Carl Boese and Paul Wegener's *The Golem*. Momentum built with F.W. Murnau's *Nosferatu* in 1922, and he pressed the case with *Faust*, five years later. In 1932, there came *Vampyr* from Danish visionary Carl Theodor Dreyer. Together, these constitute the genre's pure yet perverse opening salvo. Their effects may to the modern eye look cheap, and their scripts sound creaky, but these pioneering pictures pre-empt pop-world giants like David Lynch and David Cronenberg, causing the viewer to enter a kind of trance state with their unworldly imagery and fever-chills.

As America and Hollywood cottoned on to the genre in the 1930s, Hollywood's Universal Studios emitted landmark work from Tod Browning, Karl Freund and James Whale. In *Bride of Frankenstein* (1935) and *The Old Dark House* (1932), very different from each other, Whale made (with considerable British acting input) two of the defining gothic films. The 1940s clawed out *Cat People* (Jacques Tourneur, 1942) and its sequel, *The Curse of the Cat People* (Gunther von Fritsch, Robert Wise, 1944), both starring Simone Simon. Britain made its move with the golden era of Hammer Studios from the late 1950s, opting to depict the dark side in full-blooded colour, not black and white. By contrast, *The Innocents* (1961) was a master class in ambivalence and the power of suggestion, nudging our own imaginations to run riot.

All hell broke loose in the 1960s as Roger Corman, Stanley Kubrick, Roman Polanski and even Andy Warhol amped up the genre. Herzog hurtled forward with it while paying homage to Murnau. Moving towards modern times, monoliths like *The Exorcist* (1973), *The Wicker Man* (1973), *Suspiria* (1977) and *The Shining* (1980) pulsated with fresh-yet-morbid perspectives. Recent years have seen the *Twilight* phenomenon reboot the sex appeal of vampires, while even comic-book superhero blockbuster franchises like *Batman* are deemed shallow without a smothering sense of gloom. It seems that innovative twists or classic retellings of the Frankenstein and Dracula fables are slated for release practically every month, while the spirit of the gothic hovers in many worthy art-house films.

At the beginning of *Bride of Frankenstein*, the "pretty chills" of Mary Shelley are eulogized by Byron, before such prettiness is shown, albeit with no little camp, to be somewhat terrifying. Pretty chills abound in the glorious heritage of gothic cinema. Let us see if we can walk into the dark and face those deceptively beautiful demons.

Gothic Expression

Gothic literature had already thrived for centuries, giving us John Milton, Hugh Walpole, Lord Byron, the Shelleys (Percy Bysshe and Mary), Edgar Allan Poe, Bram Stoker and M.R. James, when the first gothic film was made in America. Most agree that this was the Edison Company's 1910 adaptation of *Frankenstein*. Yet the first film to make a serious and lasting impact was from Europe: the 1913 German silent horror film *The Student of Prague* (also known as *A Bargain with Satan*) by Hanns Heinz Ewers.

In the early years of the twentieth century, the German chatterati, reacting to the very real horrors of world war, were heatedly debating whether cinema qualified as an art form. Drawing on expressionist techniques and theatre, *The Cabinet of Dr. Caligari* (1919) proved that it did. The film's aesthetics involved fragmented narrative, striking visuals and chiaroscuro lighting. A nightmarish landscape is constructed via the use of cleverly distorted perspectives, and shadows painted on the walls and ground of the two-dimensional sets. It's arguably the true dawn of gothic cinema.

The film has influenced classic American film noir of a later period, not to mention the image and chosen subject matter of any number of Goth bands. Caligari (Werner Krauss) runs a carnival attraction, the creepy star of which is Cesare (the iconic Conrad Veidt), a sleepwalking, cadaverous type who claims to be able to see into the future. Murders occur. But, of course, things aren't quite as they seem. Cesare is a victimized monster acting out our subconscious will for revenge. As he carries his trophy Jane (Lil Dagover) over a highly stylized cityscape, many of the arch moments of gothic cinema from *King Kong* (1933) to *La Belle et La Bête* (1946) are foreshadowed. (And so was the rise of Nazism, reckoned some critics, with its menacing power-freaks duping the masses.)

A year later, in 1920, another German expressionist classic, *The Golem* (originally *Der Golem*), was promoted with a surprisingly raunchy (for its time) poster. It told a traditional Jewish fable, which Wegener had already filmed twice since 1915. This third take, subtitled *How He Came into the World*, is the defining creation. Wegener himself played the Golem, and his deliberately slow, stumbling, vaguely confused monster influenced the subsequent interpretations of Frankenstein's beast that became accepted as standard. Made from clay, the Golem is built to defend the Jews in a Prague ghetto, at the command of dark spirit Astaroth. The Golem has no soul and is worked hard, eventually

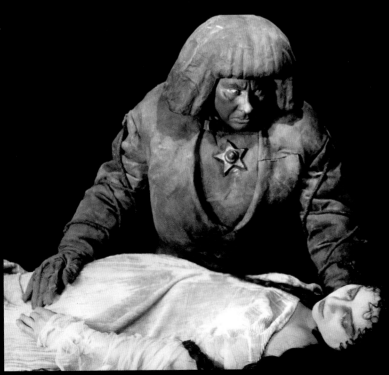

ABOVE
Cocteau's magical
La Belle et La Bête
showed that it was
possible to haunt
without horror.

LEFT
The Golem *was a*
supremely stylized
example of German
expressionism.

getting frustrated and running – or, at least, lumbering – wild. It's the film's schematic visual style that entrances. It yielded further influence on the landmark *Frankenstein* movie made by James Whale in 1931, with one scene of an innocent young girl attempting to give a rose to the monster completely copied.

In 1922, Murnau made the film that gave birth to vampire movies. *Nosferatu* remains not just the greatest silent "horror" film, but one of the pinnacles of cinema history, haunting audiences to the present day. Max Schreck's portrayal of the vampire is a far cry from Bram Stoker's descriptions. A pale, hideous, bald, hunched neo-corpse, more like a rat than a bat, with epically long fingernails/claws, jagged teeth and a chilling stare, he is the polar opposite of the "seductive" Dracula of later decades. The film was to be based on Stoker's book, but permission was denied by the novelist's widow. So Murnau and his writer changed the names of the principals – Dracula becoming Orlok, Harker becoming Hutter – and moved the tale from 1897 London to 1837 Wisborg. Mrs Stoker still sued, resulting in "all" prints being destroyed in 1925. Happily, some survived. Much later, the film was restored to its full glory and enjoyed the appreciation of generations unborn in Murnau's time. Nosferatu is one vampire who does seem to live forever. Many coming to the film for the first time will still be startled at how far Schreck detours from what became the Bela Lugosi template: "The ship of death has a new captain." His vampire is no classy aristocrat: he is grabby, desperate, a prowler who doesn't stand on ceremony. Although the film was shot across Eastern Europe, including in Transylvania, close to the castle belonging to the "actual" Dracula, the exteriors are surpassed by Schreck's sheer presence and the cruel interior silhouettes. His seminal performance has inspired homages from similarly intense actors in more recent years. Werner Herzog's 1979 remake gave Klaus Kinski his head, while Willem Dafoe doffed his cap in *Shadow of the Vampire* in 2000. Modern gothic giant *Batman Returns* (1992) even saw Christopher Walken playing a character named Max Shreck.

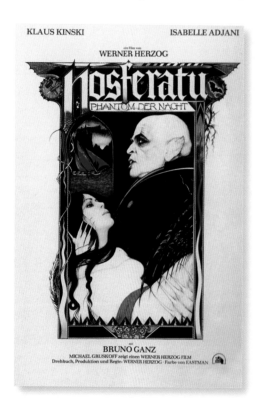

The gothic flickered through the operatic and opulent *The Phantom of the Opera* (1925) and its spectacular sets. The grand masked ball scene where the Phantom (Lon Chaney) makes his entrance in a skull-mask and scarlet cape – death incarnate – still stuns. Chaney was a pioneer of the bloodcurdling performance. His phantom sleeps in a tomb, but it is his eyes that pierce the shadows to ratchet up the fear factor. He was originally cast as Dracula in Tod

ABOVE

Bela Lugosi in Tod Browning's Dracula: *his chilling stare was boosted by ingenious lighting.*

Browning's 1931 film, which established the Count as a titan of cinema. How very different our perceptions might have been if Chaney had played the role. Instead, it was Bela Lugosi who took this particular place in gothic lore.

The Hungarian-born Lugosi reckoned the promotional material for *Dracula* "made men faint and women swoon". Modern critics often profess to be baffled by the actor's enduring legend, calling him "hammy" and "stylized", but the charisma of his accent cannot be denied. In *Dracula*, he was ably supported by Dwight Frye – later the title of an Alice Cooper track – as Renfield. Browning was a visionary American director who, along with his preferred Chaney, went on to make *Freaks* (1932), among other twisted cult films.

Dracula is, in fact, a little plodding, and yet its status as a kick-starter of a genre cannot be overplayed. Karl Freund's cinematography delivers deft moments, like the shock of the giggling lunatic on the ghost ship and the unforgettable entrance of Dracula's sleepwalking wives in their suggestive gowns. And Freund must even be given credit for one of Lugosi's best features: his enigmatic stare. If his eyes glow with a sinister light, it's because Freund aimed two compact spotlights directly into them in key scenes. For all the film's flaws, Dracula was officially here, on film, by his own name, at last – 34 years after the novel's publication. As far back as 1914, Universal Pictures had slated a Dracula movie as one of their first projects. Now, the Count was awake, and cinema would never let him go back to sleep.

The Rise of Frankenstein

OPPOSITE

A phenomenally important year for gothic cinema, 1931 also saw the emergence of Boris Karloff as Frankenstein in the seminal James Whale film.

Something of a watershed for gothic cinema, the year 1931 also gave us Fritz Lang's pessimistic masterpiece of metaphysical horror, *M*, four years after his sci-fi landmark *Metropolis*, as well as the release of James Whale's *Frankenstein*. Whale – English and the first openly gay director in Hollywood – and Browning were the leading figures in pinning the vocabulary of the period's horror films.

One Boris Karloff emerged as Whale's favoured actor, giving a touching, melancholy turn as the monster in *Frankenstein*. His creator, Dr Henry Frankenstein, played by Colin Clive, is obsessively devoted to his scientific work above all else, to the point where his wife assumes there must be another woman. But he really is working, manically. When his "monster" comes to life, Whale lifts the levels of allegory and symbolism beyond even Mary Shelley's reckonings. The monster becomes an innocent scapegoat (as does King Kong) but, at the same time, his uncomprehending innocence leads to tragedies, as when he plays with the little girl then throws her into the lake to see if she will float, only to be dismayed when she drowns.

Frankenstein is a complex film, pondering the rights and wrongs of science's urge to push boundaries and explore further. Its surface, though, is what endures, with Karloff's mournful face – the iconic make-up by Jack Pierce – a milestone on cinema's path to full maturity. The monster is more than just frightening; he is frightened, tormented, hurting, sad. He is human enough to resent the sadistic trick that Fate has played on him. He feels a pull towards evil but endeavours to resist. Can he cling on to society's embedded notions of decency and morality? Within all this lie the trace elements of what we, the audience, relate and respond to so strongly in the great darkening peaks of gothic cinema – we are all just a set of impulses away from reacting monstrously to the human condition.

Another 1931 jewel to deal symbolically with the human condition – touching on Freudian concepts - was *Dr. Jekyll and Mr. Hyde*, directed by Rouben Mamoulian and starring Fredric March. Robert Louis Stevenson's story has since become the most frequently adapted tale in the genre.

"Look! It's moving. It's alive. It's alive… it's moving. It's alive, it's alive, it's alive, it's alive!"

Dr Frankenstein in *Frankenstein* (1931)

UNIVERSAL PRESENTA
FRANKENSTEIN
CON
COLIN CLIVE
MAE CLARKE
JOHN BOLES
BORIS KARLOFF
BASADA EN LA HISTORIA de MARY WOLLSTONE CROFT SHELLEY
DIRIGIDA POR JAMES WHALE

ABOVE

*Dr Jekyll raises
a glass, darkly,
in Rouben
Mamoulian's* Dr.
Jekyll and Mr.
Hyde *from 1931.*

The early 1930s were a hugely fertile period for gothic cinema. *Vampyr*, Carl Theodor Dreyer's classic, is said to have caused the director to have a nervous breakdown; he didn't make another film for ten years. It is another very different take on vampire mythology, both in its choice of focus within the subject and its stylistic and narrative deviations from both big-studio horror and German expressionism. It's wilfully poetic and individual, forming and following the logics of dream and the unconscious. Thus it has haunted and continues to haunt, long after more obvious, visceral films have been forgotten.

The troubled, sleepwalking protagonist Allan Grey, a student of the occult, was played by Julian West, who was, in fact, one Baron Nicolas de Gunzburg, the film's financial backer. (Many of the cast were amateurs.) Grey, we are told by a helpful title card – there is little dialogue, mainly because the film had to be recorded in three languages, but don't let that spoil the mystique – is prone to getting confused as to where reality ends and the supernatural starts. He sees shadowy figures, experiences strange visitations. There follows a disorientating run of hallucinatory happenings as good fights the forces of evil, including a female vampire. Throughout, the gothic enhances the feeling of unease – such props and settings as skulls, stairwells, doppelgängers, reflections coming to life and an often mimicked book of vampire lore all but define gothic imagery. Eternal credit must go to Dreyer's cinematography team of Rudolph Maté and Louis Née, who developed such time-honoured "ghostly" tricks as double exposures, reverse-motion and shining lights at the lens to overexpose shots. "I just wanted to make a film different from all other films," said Dreyer. "I wanted, if you will, to break new ground for the cinema. That is all."

RIGHT

*The haunting and
poetic film* Vampyr,
*a flop upon its
release in 1932,
drove Carl Theodor
Dreyer, its director,
to the brink of a
nervous breakdown.*

CARL LAEMMLE
presents

The
OLD
DARK
HOUSE

from the novel by J.B. PRIESTLY
WITH
KARLOFF
MELVIN DOUGLAS
GLORIA STUART
CHARLES LAUGHTON
LILIAN BOND
ERNEST THESIGER, EVA MOORE, RAYMOND MASSEY
BREMBER WILLS, JOHN DUDGEON
Directed by
JAMES WHALE
Produced by CARL LAEMMLE JR.
A UNIVERSAL PICTURE

LEFT
The Old Dark
House *invented a
new sub-genre of
gothic cinema, to
which it effectively
lent its title. It led
to the creation of
Bates Motel in
Psycho and the
Overlook Hotel
in The Shining,
among others.*

The Old Dark House was a typical act of subversion from James Whale. Universal wanted a vehicle for Karloff, to bounce off the success of *Frankenstein*, but the director messed with expectations. Karloff and another Jack Pierce make-up masterstroke create a mesmerizing mute butler, but the ensemble (including Charles Laughton) steal Karloff's thunder somewhat. Five people take shelter in the isolated titular, decaying house on a – by necessity – dark and stormy night. The creepy, mad-as-a-box-of-snakes inhabitants, the Femm family, are more Addams family than the Waltons.

It's a black comedy of sorts, based on J.B. Priestley's 1928 novel *Benighted*, but still shocks. The gothic elements are played seriously but the eccentric characters are given left-field personalities and witty lines, almost to misdirect us. The notion of the dysfunctional family was to become a recurring device in 1970s horror. There is what later generations might call gender-bending, and one of the sons wants to burn the whole house to the ground. *The Old Dark House* is a true oddity. As critic Kim Newman has observed, its title stands in for an entire sub-genre of the gothic imagination, which has brought us the Bates Motel in *Psycho* and the Overlook Hotel in *The Shining*, among many other best-avoided locations, "inhabited by desperate characters, full of secret passageways and bricked-up rooms, haunted by spectres and guilts".

James Whale returned in 1935 with *Bride of Frankenstein*, often hailed as the campy champion of chillers. Yet it, too, is idiosyncratic, and distinguishes itself from genre clichés. Universal had persuaded Whale back to the fold by promising complete artistic freedom and a big budget. He responded with a giddy cocktail of suspense, irony, humour, pathos and fantasy, which has never been matched. With a mostly British cast, including Boris Karloff, Elsa Lanchester, teenager Valerie Hobson, Colin Clive and Dwight Frye, he created a new mood, a new kind of film. As it opens, Mary Shelley elaborates to Percy Bysshe Shelley and Lord Byron how her original tale may have continued. It's quite a vision, including a miniature Henry XIII among homunculi in glass jars. Frankenstein's monster is permitted to speak, though Karloff himself, ahead of filming, thought the decision a mistake. Now, the scene where he strives to communicate with a blind man is considered one of the era's most moving scenes, again winning sympathy for Karloff's perplexed innocent.

Elsa Lanchester played both Mary and – if ever the adjective "iconic" was justified – the monster's bride. The bride, with her unforgettable wig and make-up, physical spasms and hissing sounds, was only on screen for a matter of minutes, but has become a peerless cinematic star of gothic visuals. So enamoured of his pair of newlyweds was Whale that he let them live at the movie's end, when most other characters are wiped out amid the climactic crescendos. "We belong dead," says Karloff to Lanchester. The castle is blown up, but Mr and Mrs survive.

Island of Lost Souls (1932), with Bela Lugosi, and Kathleen Burke as Lota, the Panther Woman; *The Black Cat* (1934), with Boris Karloff and Lugosi; and the original version of *King Kong* (1933) – a twist on both the Frankenstein myth and the fairy tale *Beauty and the Beast* – also adorned the decade, soon to be followed by *The Wolf Man* in 1941, with Lon Chaney Jr. *The Hunchback of Notre Dame* (1939) saw an extraordinary performance by Charles Laughton as Quasimodo – a spiritual sibling of the beasts, surely. (In 1955, Laughton was to direct *The Night of the Hunter*, starring Robert Mitchum, which brooded in deliciously gothic style.)

OPPOSITE

Elsa Lanchester in Bride of Frankenstein. *Even though she appeared on screen for only minutes, she created one of the defining images of gothic film.*

The bells, the bells…
Charles Laughton
as Quasimodo in
The Hunchback of
Notre Dame.

Jacques Tourneur's *Cat People* (1942), made on a tight budget, echoes *Dracula* in that it is obsessed with the repression of sexual urges and has a worried fascination with Eastern Europeans. (Tourneur was to follow it in 1943 with *I Walked with a Zombie* and *The Leopard Man*.) In *Cat People*, a Serbian-born artist Irena, played by Simone Simon, sketches panthers at the zoo, day after day. Agreeing to marry a pleasant American, she then reveals to him that her village of origin was riddled with mysterious (and vague) evil. Thus, she explains, she should not sleep with him. To a psychiatrist, she confesses she is descended from "cat people", women who kill their lovers. As she genuinely loves her husband, she has a problem. Violence and dread ensue. The film's success ensured a follow-up, *The Curse of the Cat People*, in which Simon played Irena's ghost. The shadows and fear in these two classics are mainly in the mind. In 1982, Paul Schrader directed a remake of *Cat People*, with Nastassja Kinski, which was more explicit about the sexual aspect, yet also maintained a strange, suspenseful, almost tactile allure.

"One of the most magical of all films," said the film critic Roger Ebert of Jean Cocteau's *La Belle et La Bête*, going on to describe a beast who – like Frankenstein's – is "lonely like a man and misunderstood like an animal". If the poet's fabulous, baroque 1946 film is not scary or "horror" as such, it is gothic romance on the most elevated plane. Beast (Jean Marais) proposes marriage to Beauty (Josette Day) nightly. She refuses but eventually a trust develops. He allows her home to visit her family, with an enchanted key and glove, saying that if she chooses not to return within a week, he will die of sadness. In a convoluted, bitter-sweet ending, Beast both dies and is reborn as Prince Ardent.

In the film's prologue, Cocteau writes: "Children believe what we tell them. They have complete faith in us. They believe that a rose plucked from a garden can plunge a family into conflict. They believe that the hands of a human beast will smoke when he slays a victim, and that this will cause him shame when a young maiden takes up residence in his home. They believe a thousand other simple things." The willing suspension of disbelief remains a key factor in our relish – as adults – of otherworldly, gothic films. The beauty-and-the-beast allegory has, of course, been reworked and reimagined in many different periods and milieus.

WITH
SIMONE SIMON
KENT SMITH
TOM CONWAY
JANE RANDOLPH
JACK HOLT

Produced by VAL LEWTON
Directed by JACQUES TOURNEUR
Written by DeWitt Bodeen

A REGAL FILMS INTERNATIONAL RELEASE

Schlock Horror

The European "art-house" sensibility explored by Cocteau and Tourneur also informed *Les Diaboliques* (1955), directed by Henri-Georges Clouzot. (Alfred Hitchcock had wanted to buy the rights but lost out by just a few hours and ending up making *Vertigo* (1958) instead.) *Les Diaboliques* shook mass audiences, just when they thought it was safe to go back in the bathroom. Britain had served notice of intent with *Dead of Night* in 1945, a portmanteau horror from Ealing Studios. Now, however, the British really were coming… "to haunt you forever", as the poster to the first major Hammer breakthrough, *The Curse of Frankenstein*, boasted in 1956. And we entered the garishly coloured age of Peter Cushing, Vincent Price and Christopher Lee. Universal's era of dominance had eaten itself in an excess of sequels, franchise-crossovers and copycats – how very like today! Horror movies had fallen out of fashion for years. Along came Hammer to strike a blow for anti-nature and schlock, and revive the genre. The British press were, however, not impressed. In fact they were appalled. The *Observer* called Terence Fisher's film, which starred Cushing and Lee, "among the half-dozen most repulsive films I have ever encountered". The public, on the other hand, flocked to see the gore and torn-off limbs (and Frankenstein's monster taking an acid bath). Within a year, Hammer and Fisher had bashed out a Cushing-and-Lee version of *Dracula* (also known as *Horror of Dracula*), which was an international smash, and

RIGHT

Henri-Georges Clouzot's uncompromising film Diabolique *(originally* Les Diaboliques*) made audiences afraid of their bath-tubs.*

their subsequent run of Dracula movies would extend into the 1970s. The use of colour was crucial to their success: coffins spattered with crimson blood thrilled viewers. Fisher also realized the value of close-ups as Lee's Dracula sank his fangs into compliant necks, his eyes turning red as he drank.

Dracula may be ageless but gothic horror was now established in the colour age. Hammer ran and ran with it: raining blood and heaving bosoms everywhere. The controversial ending of Fisher's *Dracula, Prince Of Darkness* (1965) – vampire lesbianism and hammer-and-stake murders – was either its zenith or its nadir. Italian gothic, too, hiring Christopher Lee, gathered momentum, although early on its aesthetic leaned towards a more lofty eroticism than the titillating cackling-and-cleavages of Hammer. *Mask of the Demon* (1960), directed by Mario Bava, all vengeful witches and a fixation on Barbara Steele's eyes, marked the start of its most creative phase. The provocatively libidinous qualities of Hammer horror and Italian gothic upset prudes, placated

ABOVE

Vampire's kiss:
Christopher Lee
embraces the
Hammer horror
of Dracula.

mass audiences and were defended by aesthetes as being true to the subversive essence of gothicism. Bava and the Italian "giallo" movement, which influenced Dario Argento, lurched then into lurid colours and flamboyant violence, usually against women in crypts and castles. Bava's notorious *Black Sabbath* (1963) used Boris Karloff as a resonant elder statesman.

Before the 1960s beckoned in this more promiscuous sensibility, *Eyes Without a Face* (1959) by Georges Franju was perhaps the last great tingler. Originally titled *Les Yeux Sans Visage*, it emerged roughly around the same time as Michael Powell's daring *Peeping Tom* (1960) and Hitchcock's *Psycho* (1960), and all three were loudly condemned as beyond the pale. Mixing B-movie staples with poetic high art, *Eyes Without a Face* was a thinly veiled criticism of Nazism. Dr Génessier (Pierre Brasseur) carries a veneer of sophistication, under which beats a cold, unfeeling heart and demented sociopathy. He wants to beautify the face of his daughter, disfigured during a car crash, so he kidnaps and kills young female students, trying to graft their skin onto hers. His hideous experiments ring with echoes of history's atrocities. In the States, the film was retitled *The Horror Chamber of Dr Faustus*.

While the work of the great Alfred Hitchcock is effectively now its own genre, he has, of course, overlapped with the gothic on many occasions. Bates Motel in *Psycho* is arguably the ultimate "old dark house", and many of its images have become shorthand for "scary movies". It's a psychodrama as much as a meta-melodrama, its intensity heightened by Bernard Herrmann's musical flourishes. One feels for the late Anthony Perkins, his promising acting career hamstrung after this by being typecast as creepy, twitchy voyeur Norman.

Three years on, Hitchcock's *The Birds* (1963) was released. This adaptation of a Daphne du Maurier story – Hitchcock had also filmed *Rebecca* (1940) based on her classic gothic novel of the same name – gave Tippi Hedren a tough time as the internal terrors of *Psycho* evolved into a real and vivid external threat. While the birds gradually build in number and menace and volume, attacking indiscriminately, they assume powerfully resonant symbolic authority as arch agents of the gothic.

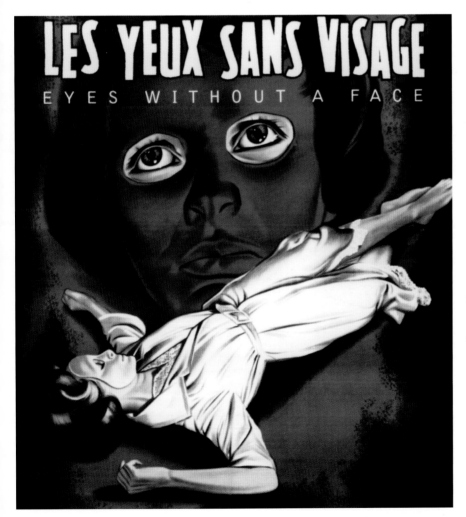

LEFT

The shocking surgical experiments in Eyes Without a Face *caused audience members to faint. One enraged critic suggested Georges Franju, the film's director, be burned at the stake.*

Psychological Trauma

Originally advertised as "a strange new experience in shock", the recently rereleased *The Innocents*, directed by Jack Clayton, is not a typical fright night, but has lingered as one of the outstanding gothic pictures ever since it won Palme d'Or and BAFTA nominations in 1961. Based on Henry James's turn-of-the-century novella *The Turn of the Screw* (adapted by William Archibald and one Truman Capote), it skilfully attains the story's ambiguity and carefully calibrated twist into the supernatural – or what might be the insane delusions of governess Miss Giddens (Deborah Kerr). Clayton leaves us to decide whether she is killing or curing. The children in her charge are confident, sinister; the apparitions – welcomed or not by the children – terrifyingly ambivalent. Even the sounds of the film, the wind in the trees, spook us. A contender as the greatest of ghost films, entirely earnest and devoid of ironic distancing, *The Innocents* leaves most of the

work to our imaginations. And our imaginations, as the gothic nurtures and capitalizes on time and time again, are willing grafters. As Michael Newton wrote in The *Guardian*, "*The Innocents* is a film that infiltrates and celebrates the imagination, while recognizing that faculty's pitfalls. For, it argues, while the imaginative may understand situations and people better, sometimes, to their and our danger, they see rather more than is there."

Herk Harvey's artful *Carnival of Souls* (1962) centres on an amusement park, where a young woman (Candace Hilligoss), who thinks she's survived a car crash, finds herself in a dance with the dead. It influenced George A. Romero's later head-on zombie horrors, such as *Night of the Living Dead* (1969). King of the low-budget flick Roger Corman made his mark on the gothic with his "Poe cycle", which included *House of Usher* (1960) and *The Pit and the Pendulum* (1961),

"Waking a child can sometimes be worse than any bad dream."

Mrs Grose in *The Innocents* (1961)

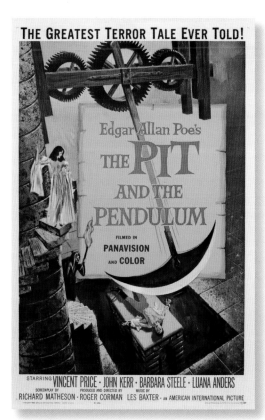

but arguably peaked with *The Masque of the Red Death* (1964), boasting luxuriant cinematography by the great Nicolas Roeg. Poe is as gothic as gothic gets, but Corman manages to squeeze in extra existentialism, satanism and wit. Vincent Price throws himself into the role of Prince Prospero, who even Satan cannot defend from the contagion assaulting his land. Neither can hedonistic parties in his castle. Questioning God, Prospero shouts, "Famine, pestilence, war, disease and death – they rule this world!" A scarlet-clad reaper appears and tells him, as if informing us of a gothic aesthetic, "Man creates his own God, his own Heaven, his own Hell. This is your Hell."

The intersection between outer demons and inner trauma is again probed in Roman Polanski's best work (which doesn't include *The Fearless Vampire Killers*). *Repulsion* (1965) echoes *The Innocents* or *The Birds*, with its leading lady's withdrawal into nightmare and hallucination. Catherine Deneuve's Carol is followed around London by the camera's male gaze as she descends – as it all but cruelly wills her to – into psychosis. Deneuve portrays the emotional push and pull of her increasing distress quite brilliantly. As she neurotically shuts out the world, we become complicit accomplices in imagining the worst until, inevitably, it happens. In *Rosemary's Baby* (1968), Polanski more overtly embraces horror tropes, but again analyses the submissive role foisted upon women by "respectable" society. Satanists indoctrinate pregnant Rosemary (Mia Farrow);

ABOVE LEFT

Vincent Price starred in a number of Roger Corman's lurid Edgar Allan Poe adaptations, including The Pit and the Pendulum...

ABOVE RIGHT

... and The Masque of the Red Death. *With cinematography by Nicolas Roeg, this was the most acclaimed.*

her husband, it transpires, has made a pact with them. Catholic rituals are targeted too as the film grows increasingly grotesque. When Rosemary sees her baby (we, importantly, don't), she screams. Of course, it might all be a nightmare, but by now we've learned from gothic cinema that it might not. In his creative heyday, Polanski kept the plates of uncertainty spinning and quivering with a conjurer's guile.

Terence Fisher and Christopher Lee returned in 1968 with *The Devil Rides Out* (US title: *The Devil's Bride*), based on Dennis Wheatley's occult novel. Aleister Crowley had been Wheatley's "consultant" some decades earlier, and Wheatley had based the satanic figure Mocata (played juicily in the film by Charles Gray) on him. Fisher directed with more vigour than ever. Lee, atypically, plays the good guy, trying to thwart the villainous Mocata and his sect with white magic. Until the throw-in-the-kitchen-sink climax, this is a superior, unusually sophisticated Hammer film.

The beauty of woman— the demon of darkness— the unholy union of "The Devil's Bride"!

20th CENTURY-FOX presents

THE DEVIL'S BRIDE

COLOR by DeLUXE

starring
CHRISTOPHER LEE
CHARLES GRAY
NIKE ARRIGHI · LEON GREENE
also starring PATRICK MOWER · GWEN FFRANGCON-DAVIES
SARAH LAWSON · PAUL EDDINGTON
Screenplay by RICHARD MATHESON · From the Novel "The Devil Rides Out" by DENNIS WHEATLEY
Produced by ANTHONY NELSON KEYS · Directed by TERENCE FISHER · A Seven Arts-Hammer Film Production

Move to Mainstream

The 1970s saw Hammer running out of steam and, after one-off oddities like the bizarre spoof *The Abominable Dr. Phibes* (1971), Nicolas Roeg's challenging, haunting *Don't Look Now* (1973) and the "classy" Belgian lesbian vampire cult favourite *Daughters of Darkness* (1970), Hollywood howled back to the forefront. The pomp and gory glory of Hammer and Corman were overpowered by the modern, more "gritty" horrors of chainsaw-maniacs and Romero's zombies. Wes Craven's *The Last House on the Left* (1972) served up extended graphic scenes of merciless torture. A year later came the massively popular, game-changing *The Exorcist*, the first horror film to be nominated for a Best Picture Oscar.

The Exorcist was perhaps the first gross-out film to eschew low-budget traditions and hire the best effects available. Its other flash of inspiration was to get William Friedkin to direct. Having proven he could do earthy realism in *The French Connection* (1971), he now fixed the Catholic terrors of this money-spinner (and head-spinner) within a credible family in the present-day world. Polanski had done this in *Rosemary's Baby*. Likewise, *The Exorcist* took itself and its audience seriously. Its plot is minimal, but ghastly: demonic forces possess a girl, Regan (Linda Blair), and exorcists battle for her soul. She vomits, blasphemes and masturbates, leaving future parodists with an easy target and

RIGHT

Nicolas Roeg brought a profound, melancholy poetry to his film Don't Look Now, *from 1973.*

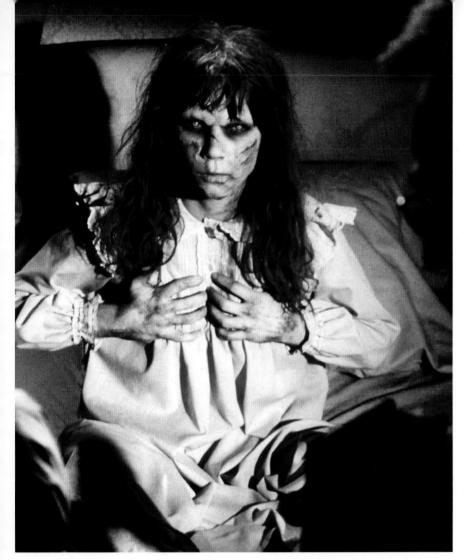

leaving the viewer with an ambiguous ending. The pacing lures you into an urban drama before pulverizing you with the jolts.

It was the biggest film of 1973, and boosted sales of Mike Oldfield's album *Tubular Bells*, which featured on the soundtrack. The all-conquering tsunami of the much-imitated *The Exorcist* may seem hard to comprehend nowadays, especially when compared to the more layered scares of that year's *Don't Look Now* or the evergreen insanity of *The Wicker Man*, but it completely rebooted the genre. "A thoroughly evil film," wrote critic Andrew Sarris.

The Wicker Man, directed by Robin Hardy and written by Anthony Shaffer, is another of the great one-offs in gothic cult-film history and, outside of Hammer, the most British. It begins deceptively as a police case, with Edward Woodward's devoutly Christian, buttoned-up copper arriving on a remote Scottish island in search of a missing girl. We are misdirected from the true pagan nature of the situation by sunny daylight and a music soundtrack of

traditional folk. Atmosphere and language do not instantly suggest the gothic. Christopher Lee's Lord Summerisle says of (Christianity's) God: "He's dead… had his chance and, in modern parlance, blew it." Yet the film, once described in America as "the *Citizen Kane* of horror movies", progresses into a unique fusion of the mysterious, the erotic and, ultimately, with its famous twist ending, the nightmarish. Despite a misfiring Neil LaBute remake in 2006, *The Wicker Man* burns on, with Christopher Lee naming it as his best film. Accompanied by *Witchfinder General* (1968) and *Blood on Satan's Claw* (1971), it is the pinnacle of British Folk Gothic, though, like all the most enduring films, it tends to mean different things to different people.

    Jaws (1975), *Carrie* (1976), *The Omen* (1976) and *Halloween* (1978) further popularized horror through the mid- to late 1970s, but the next undisputed gothic masterpiece emanated from Italy. Dario Argento's *Suspiria* (1977) was a gruesome fairy tale in which a naïve young woman, played by Jessica Harper, faces peril in Germany in the form of a coven of witches. Argento – also the director of *Profondo Rosso* (1975) and *Inferno* (1980) – doesn't present the supernatural with a fanfare: he plunges her (and us) directly into a whirlpool of the subconscious, bombarding us with treated technicolour visuals and an aggressive soundtrack from Goblin. Bat attacks are a gothic standard, but Argento hurls in stabbings, hangings and the undead Mother of Whispers. Demented and disturbing, *Suspiria* is, for all its symphonic palette, as dark as dark gets.

If *Suspiria* forged new shapes, Werner Herzog's *Nosferatu the Vampyre* (1979), set in nineteenth-century Transylvania and Germany, was a hypnotic homage to the Murnau film, which pretty much started it all – Herzog considered it the greatest film ever to emerge from Germany. Stylish, meditative and given wings by Wagner, it both reveres and magnifies its source, keen on mood rather than shocks. Bravely, given how far towards dashing and seductive the populist image of vampires had evolved, it echoes and eulogizes the earlier film's focus on the vampire as ugly, lonely, love-starved, forlorn: a rodent. Immortality brings him only the despair of purgatory. Bats play a big role, with one haunting Lucy's (Isabelle Adjani) nightmare at the opening of the film. However, it's the performance of long-time Herzog ally Klaus Kinski that lingers. Obviously inspired by Max Schreck (and four-hour make-up sessions), he blends physical discomfort with philosophical angst.

Around this time, David Lynch was rising to prominence. The bewildering and unsettling *Eraserhead* (1977) pirouetted on the line between nightmare and reality, using surrealism and flickering light to throw us off in its industrial gothic monochrome dreamscape. Three years later *The Elephant Man*, with John Hurt as the unfortunate John Merrick, found critical and commercial success. "I am not

ABOVE
"Here's Johnny!"
The Shining
*(1980), starring
Jack Nicholson and
Shelley Duvall, saw
Stanley Kubrick in
typically perverse,
challenging form.*

an elephant, I am not an animal!" he cries as he is threatened by a mob. "I am a human being! I am a man!" Merrick represents in some ways a more real, more articulate Frankenstein's monster, and suffers similarly. Lynch has gone on to redefine the narrative routing and acceptability of the dream logic of film, in such compelling curveballs as *Blue Velvet* (1986) and *Lost Highway* (1997).

Stanley Kubrick swam between genres in his career but struck the mother lode of suspense and horror in *The Shining* (1980), which glorifies the gothic in its location (the ominous, isolated hotel – an old dark house, anyone?), its score (Gregorian chants) and the Poe-like manner in which Jack Torrance's (Jack Nicholson) psyche grows warped. It's not until 90 minutes in that we get the legendary cry of "Here's Johnny!" and the axe crashing through the door as he pursues his wife and child. Fuelled by dread of what's to come and punctuated with indelible images such as the vision of the dead girls, *The Shining*, based on Stephen King's novel, is aglow with palpable tension.

BELOW
Kubrick claimed he took the tone of The Shining *from the writings of Franz Kafka. The sense of dread that the film conveys builds to an ominous pitch.*

Glossy Gothic

As the 1980s grew in gloss (and ground-breaking make-up from Rick Baker), Brian De Palma constructed Hitchcock homages, werewolves enjoyed a renaissance in such films as *The Howling* (1980) and *An American Werewolf in London* (1981), and *Poltergeist* (1982) upped the ante on terrorized children and haunted-house effects. *The Hunger* (1983), directed by Tony Scott, was the ultimate 1980s vampire film, bringing a topical, shiny sensibility to its tale of photogenic lesbians (Catherine Deneuve, Susan Sarandon) and jaded immortals (David Bowie). Dismissed as flashy and near-pornographic on release, its bravura opening (Bauhaus sing "Bela Lugosi's Dead" over a libidinous nightclub scene) and tragic ending (Deneuve doomed to reside in a coffin pleading for her lover, forever) have earned the film a camp-sincere crossover following. A far cry from Max Schreck, it certainly played its part in "sexing up" vampires, as did the 1987 pair *The Lost Boys* (Joel Schumacher) and *Near Dark* (Kathryn Bigelow).

In realizing Angela Carter's werewolf story, Neil Jordan's *The Company of Wolves* (1984) found a mid-point between poetic sensitivity and Hammer-like sensationalism. Roger Ebert called it a "disturbing and stylish attempt to collect some of the nightmares that lie beneath the surface of 'Little Red Riding Hood'". The irrepressible Ken Russell gave us the curio *Gothic* (1986), based on the Shelleys' visit with Byron to Villa Diodati near Lake Geneva. Gabriel Byrne plays Byron, Julian Sands is Percy Bysshe Shelley, Natasha Richardson is Mary.

OPPOSITE

Deneuve, Sarandon and Bowie played a major part in the canny "sexing up" of vampires in The Hunger *(1983).*

BELOW

The Howling *(1981) was Joe Dante's knowing revival of the werewolf genre. It spawned six sequels.*

Imagine your worst fear a reality.

THE HOWLING

A DANIEL H. BLATT PRODUCTION "THE HOWLING" starring DEE WALLACE · PATRICK MACNEE · DENNIS DUGAN · CHRISTOPHER STONE · BELINDA BALASKI · KEVIN McCARTHY · JOHN CARRADINE SLIM PICKENS And introducing ELISABETH BROOKS Executive Producers DANIEL H. BLATT and STEVEN A. LANE Screenplay by JOHN SAYLES and TERENCE H. WINKLESS Based on the novel by GARY BRANDNER Music by PINO DONAGGIO Produced by MICHAEL FINNELL and JACK CONRAD Directed by JOE DANTE Presented by AVCO EMBASSY INTERNATIONAL FILM INVESTORS and MECOM PRODUCTIONS ORIGINAL MOTION PICTURE SOUNDTRACK ALBUM AVAILABLE ON SABRE GARDANCE RECORDS AVCO EMBASSY PICTURES Release

As they egg each other on to write a horror story, with Mary coming up trumps, the beginnings of the genre are examined and romanticized, and Russell breathlessly plays fast and loose with history, as only he could.

The tills of the cinema mainstream now rang to the overt gore of Wes Craven, Sam Raimi and Clive Barker as we moved towards the 1990s, though David Cronenberg toyed with expectations in *The Fly* (1986). *The Silence of the Lambs* (1990) and Anthony Hopkins' Hannibal Lecter proved an Oscar-magnet. Was the intoxicating Victorian cocktail of sex-and-death out for the count? No chance. "Love Never Dies," declared the posters in 1992 as Francis Ford Coppola exhumed the Dark Prince in the awkwardly titled *Bram Stoker's Dracula*. The vampire is here redrafted as a tragic, somewhat noble hero, who has renounced God because his wife's suicide led to her being damned by the Church. Four centuries later she is reincarnated in London, and their reunion brings redemption. Gary Oldman shovels on the violent passions, and Coppola

eschews CGI, using only historic methods of illusion. The costumes are a bizarre hybrid of authentic period and modern "Goth". "In the presence of a vampire," shrugged the director, "all the rules of physics would be off."

Few modern directors have been labelled gothic as often as Tim Burton, yet there is something of the flamboyant circus-showman in his (usually) primary-coloured work, which argues against this. Hits like *Beetlejuice* (1988), *Edward Scissorhands* (1990), *Corpse Bride* (2005) and *Dark Shadows* (2012) undoubtedly manoeuvre, mischievously, within the genre. *Sleepy Hollow* (1999), with its production design heavily influenced by Burton's admiration for Hammer, was mock-grotesque. Starring regular Burton co-conspirator Johnny Depp, it was a huge hit, with its graveyards, supernatural flourishes and Headless Horseman. Despite this, one critic dismissed it as "little more than a lavish, art-directed slasher movie". In 2007, Burton helmed the big-budget film version of the Stephen Sondheim-Hugh Wheeler musical *Sweeney Todd: The Demon Barber of Fleet Street*, a Victorian melodrama about the serial killer who made meat pies from his corpses. *Mamma Mia!* it wasn't, and Depp's singing drew mixed reactions. It's been reported that Burton may soon remake "The Addams Family", based on the original cartoons, which should suit his wry take on the gothic perfectly.

His rendition of *Batman Returns* (1992) took the caped crusader into gloomier areas than he'd previously inhabited, and eased the path of the next remake. "There was this big backlash that I was too dark," said Burton. When Christopher Nolan took over the franchise from 2005 onwards, the world was ready for a murkier Batman, as played by Christian Bale. *Batman Begins* (2005), *The Dark Knight* (2008) and *The Dark Knight Rises* (2012) proved to be among the most commercially successful films of all time. Of *The Dark Knight*, with its memorable portrayal of The Joker by the late Heath Ledger, Ebert wrote, "A haunted film that leaps beyond its origins and becomes an engrossing tragedy." Hailed as the decade's most exciting blockbuster, it was *The Dark Knight* that confirmed that modern audiences were more than willing to enter dark nights of the soul with their heroes and anti-heroes. The gothic was now no longer a cult of the occult: in the twenty-first century, it was the Everyday.

There were pitch-black thrillers such as David Fincher's *Seven* (1995), voyeuristic mockumentaries (*The Blair Witch Project*, brilliantly hyped in 1999, shook the line between reality and fiction, ushering in the new everybody-is-a-film-maker age), and feminist re-shapings: *Ginger Snaps* (2000) saw lycanthropy as a metaphor for the burgeoning sexual awareness of adolescent girls, foreshadowing *Jennifer's Body* (2009). Alejandro Amenábar's *The Others* (2001), an impeccably executed homage to *The Innocents*, featuring commitment and restraint from Nicole Kidman that matched Deborah Kerr's, judged its pace and revelations (in another old dark house) flawlessly.

With vampires and the supernatural now dominating TV drama aimed at younger, hipper audiences – after the crucial breakthrough of Joss Whedon's brilliant "Buffy the Vampire Slayer" and "Angel", which cracked jokes about the apocalypse but still made you care – the scares became multi-layered. "True Blood", "Dexter" and recently "American Horror Story" have shuffled and subverted the staples of sex, gore and shocks. The temperature was thus set for the teen-bait catnip of the *Twilight* films, based on Stephenie Meyer's books, which from their 2008 debut have slain box offices around the world. Under stormy skies, 17-year-old Bella (Kristen Stewart) falls for Edward (Robert Pattinson) at school. A model of restraint, this vampire drinks only animal blood and warns her to stay away from him. As the franchise develops across *New Moon* (2009) and *Eclipse* (2010), the pair struggle to deny their overpowering love for each other. As Pattinson became the heart-throb of a swooning generation of females, one had to remember what a long, long way the popular notion of the vampire had travelled from "hideous" Nosferatu and campy counts.

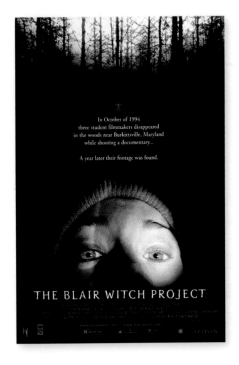

In October of 1994 three student filmmakers disappeared in the woods near Burkittsville, Maryland while shooting a documentary...

A year later their footage was found.

THE BLAIR WITCH PROJECT

Fusing Art and Exploitation

Having cleaned up at the cash register, the gothic was again being embraced by Academy Award-nominated films. Darren Aronofsky's psychological-horror *Black Swan* (2010), starring an Oscar-winning Natalie Portman, choreographed *Swan Lake* as a living, schizophrenic nightmare, echoing the spirit of Polanski's *Repulsion*. And when Daniel Radcliffe wanted to prove himself as an adult actor after growing up through the record-breaking *Harry Potter* franchise (which itself served up a swag-bag of gothic settings and elements), it was acclaimed, Edwardian-set, ghost story *The Woman in Black* (2012) in which he did so. In fact, the critical consensus called it "traditional to a fault", suggesting it "forwent gore for chills", and might not appease audiences now attuned to the excesses of the likes

ABOVE AND OPPOSITE

Roman Polanski's Repulsion *(1965) evoked schizophrenic nightmares, fusing a vulnerable woman's inner and outer realities, as did Darren Aronofsky's* Black Swan, *which starred Natalie Portman, 45 years later.*

RIGHT

The Woman in Black *(2012), the Edwardian era ghost story, brought Hammer, the studio behind the film, back to the box office big time.*

WHAT DID THEY SEE?

FEBRUARY 2012
WOMANINBLACK.COM

of horror-frenzy *Saw* (2004). Yet, with a 12A certificate, *The Woman in Black* was the highest-grossing British horror film in two decades. And the studio behind it? The revived Hammer, bought by a Dutch media tycoon in 2007. "The brand is still alive, but no one has invested in it for a long time," he said.

With Hammer emerging proudly from its coffin – *Let Me In* (2010), a remake of surprise Swedish art-house vampire-romance hit *Let the Right One In* (2008), and *The Resident* (2010) have also wowed crowds – gothic cinema is in rude health. *Berberian Sound Studio* (2012), a stylized, nerve-shredding twist on Italian "giallo" gothic, set in a claustrophobic 1970s horror film studio, was hailed as one of the best films of recent years. The icons now come at us from all angles, reinvented in increasingly warped and wonderful ways – even Abraham

Lincoln hunts vampires. Inspired by the *Underworld* franchise, in which vampires battled werewolves, the absurd *I, Frankenstein* (2014) sees a now heroic immortal "Adam Frankenstein" (formerly the Monster) fighting demons, aided by gargoyle queens. Jonathan Glazer's *Under the Skin* (2013) is a sci-fi thriller that casts Scarlett Johansson as an alluring alien hitchhiker who propels the sex-and-death equation to new levels of deranged glamour. Jim Jarmusch's *Only Lovers Left Alive* (2013) focuses on a debauched romance between "wise but fragile outsiders" that has lasted many centuries, but they're finding modern times in Detroit and Tangier a bit hard to handle. It seems the modern vampire can go anywhere as long as he or she looks dashing while doing so.

Today, having survived decades of marginalization, gothic cinema has learned to fuse art and exploitation, to co-exist and breed with the mainstream, alert, as ever, to the fact that sex and romance ("pretty chills") can sell anything, even death. It's a dream, draping our psyches with seductive shadows, from which we refuse to wake up. It's alive.

BELOW

Jim Jarmusch's Only Lovers Left Alive *(2013), with Tilda Swinton and Tom Hiddleston, is proof that the vampire movie, in various guises, lives forever.*

"The children of the night,
what sweet music they make!"

**Count Dracula, in *Bram Stoker's Dracula*,
1992, directed by Francis Ford Coppola**

MUSIC

PREVIOUS PAGE

*None more Goth:
The Cure onstage
in Rotterdam,
1985. To this day,
the band draw a
feverishly devoted
fan following.*

OPPOSITE

*"The ungodly
godfather of Goth":
high-cheekboned
Peter Murphy of
Bauhaus sang "Bela
Lugosi's Dead".*

THE WIND howled as I wended my way along the cracked, lonely road to interview former Bauhaus frontman Peter Murphy, and clouds the colour of ravens haunted the bruised sky. Upon arrival at the hotel with its ominous facade, the concierge, taciturn, unblinking, directed me to the elevator, which glided relentlessly upwards. I negotiated a corridor, as dark as day allows, its countless secrets withheld. I knocked on Murphy's door, the man once known as "the godfather of Goth". There was no response; the silence was that of a centuries-old tomb. My heart beat like the wings of a giant crow. Sticking my courage to the mast, I knocked once again. The door creaked slowly open. Murphy, who had been sleeping the sleep of the just, poked his pale head out, his eyes piercing the gloom. He breathed deeply. "Oh, right, yeah, the interview," he said. "I'll be down in a minute, mate. Meet me in reception, yeah?"

The gothic does not die. It lives eternal. But when did gothic music begin? That is something of a grey, rather than jet-black, area. Working class, from Stoke-on-Trent, Havergal Brian (1876–1972) was a prolific classical music composer. He was neglected for most of his long life until the 1950s and 1960s saw him start to be appreciated, at least for his output – he wrote no less than 32 symphonies. In 1961, his *Symphony No. 1 in D Minor*, also known as "The Gothic", was first performed in an amateur production at Westminster Central Hall. By 1966, it had been performed by professionals at the Royal Albert Hall, and broadcast live by the BBC. Then aged 90, Brian was present to take a bow, but although he was no longer a complete unknown, his work never achieved true crossover popularity. According to *Guinness World Records*, "The Gothic" is the longest symphony ever composed, but the claim is disputed. There is much of the epic, the monumental, about the work, as it addresses humanity and spirituality.

"My name is Lucifer, please take my hand," sings Ozzy Osbourne on Black Sabbath's eponymous 1970 debut album, sometimes called "the greatest metal album of all time". Like Havergal Brian, the Birmingham hard-rockers have been cited as the inventors of gothic music, but worthwhile arguments can also be presented for The Velvet Underground, Nico, Leonard Cohen, even Alice Cooper (once described as "the ungodly godfather of Goth"). Some would suggest The Doors with their track "The End", or the darker prog-rock emissions of early Genesis or Pink Floyd. Iggy Pop's album *The Idiot*, created with David Bowie, wins the vote of others.

Yet as far back as 1937, blues man Robert Johnson was singing of Faustian pacts and hellhounds on his trail. Gene Vincent raced with the devil in 1956, while Screamin' Jay Hawkins and The Crazy World of Arthur Brown pre-empted shock rock in the following decade. (We'll skip over "Monster Mash", recorded by Bobby "Boris" Pickett & The Crypt-Kickers, which was banned by the BBC as "too morbid" in 1962, but a top three hit 11 years later.) Even earlier, Stravinsky's *Firebird* terrified audiences in 1911, and Tchaikovsky's *Swan Lake* (1876) certainly has its chilling moments. Carl Orff's cantata *Carmina Burana*

(1935) is nothing if not ominous. Folk music, meanwhile, has a centuries-long tradition of uncompromising murder ballads. It stands to reason that getting any two people to agree on when and where gothic music began won't be easy. What can be confirmed, however, is that it persists and endures, despite being declared dead many times. And there's little more definitively gothic than that.

"Goth" music is a dominant sub-sect, a powerful subculture, a different beast, generally perceived to have proliferated during a specific era, the 1980s, though its long tail still swishes. Major players like The Cure, Joy Division, The Damned and Siouxsie and the Banshees had arrived before then, but a convenient calling-card for the genre is Bauhaus' first single, "Bela Lugosi's Dead", released in August 1979. And thus the best part of a decade saw the primary colours and visual positivity of Wham!, Culture Club and The Human League countered by the wilfully morose, melancholy offerings of The Sisters of Mercy, The Birthday Party, Cocteau Twins, The Mission and many more. Those feeling young and alienated at the time could don black and relate to Goth's revelatory subtext of a manifesto: it's all futile, everything is pointless, death (not love) conquers all. Destruction, pain and insecurity were the new teen angst.

Although it stuck like the flour on the clothes of Fields of the Nephilim, the name "Goths" technically didn't fit the followers of this music, who were mostly gentle, sensitive souls. Were they an ancient German tribe who disgusted the swanky Romans with their barbaric ways? No. Were they reminiscent of a form of medieval architecture? They were not. However, The Doors had been described as "gothic rock" by critic John Stickney in 1967, and the term gathered traction. In 1979, producer Martin Hannett referenced Joy Division as "dancing music with gothic overtones"; their loquacious manager Tony Wilson labelled them "gothic" on his TV show "Something Else". Within a year, *Melody Maker* described the band as "masters of this gothic gloom". Their album *Closer* had previously seen *Sounds* magazine acclaiming "dark strokes of gothic rock". And it was *Sounds'* Steve Keaton who, noting the audience at a UK Decay gig, wrote the 1981 article "The Face of Punk Gothique", asking, "Could this be the coming of Punk Gothique? With Bauhaus flying in on similar wings, could it be the next big thing?"

The opening of The Batcave club in London's Soho in July 1982 gave the growing movement a nocturnal meeting-and-bonding point. "Goths", "Batcavers", "positive punks" – the phraseology could be debated, but the tribe had assembled. The "genre" was established. There were, of course, a few hammy-horror bandwagon-jumpers, so every band that became associated with it spent most of their interviews telling the press it didn't want to be pigeon-holed, and denying their Goth-ness. Even Joy Division asserted they were the opposite of "gloomy". There was laconic, self-effacing humour evident among some of the genre's anti-stars. In 1987, Robert Smith of The Cure told me, "I stare into mirrors and I hypnotize myself to see the devil in my face and skull." OK, maybe you had to be there. Yet the dawn of Goth still represents the dark heart and burnt-gold age of what the world best knows as gothic music. While the wings of the umbrella term span far and wide, backwards and forwards in time, the great Goth era remains its grandiose central station.

Its legacy fuelled later resurgences, best represented by such successes as Marilyn Manson, Nine Inch Nails and elements of the emo movement. The gothic's blood runs on from Joy Division's muttered "… you cry out in your sleep" to Bullet for My Valentine's shrieked "The only way out is to die". Soft Cell made "sex music for gargoyles". Nick Cave, on *Murder Ballads*, sang lines like, "She'd been stabbed repeatedly and stuffed into a sleeping bag." And even if the rock tropes were replaced by trip hop, there were Grand Guignol facets to the emotional charge of Portishead or Björk. Even Ozzy's daughter Kelly Osbourne said, "I hate the word gothic, but I would like to try doing something like that. A gothic sound – not rock, but gothic. There's a difference."

Perennially thrilling, the gothic isn't going away any time soon.

RIGHT

*This last night in
Sodom: Soft Cell
(Marc Almond
and David Ball)
perform on TV show
"The Tube".*

My Name is Lucifer

Black Sabbath stumbled on a new genre when they – some might say ham-fistedly and accidentally – twisted traditional blues rock into something darker, louder and uglier. When the track "N.I.B." on *Black Sabbath* prompted jester-fool-seer Ozzy Osbourne to test a few taboos and holler, "My name is Lucifer, please take my hand," the rock audience felt a frisson of nervous intoxication. Just as Iggy and The Stooges' broken glass had led to unsightly bleeding all over the Moroccan rugs of America's 1960s hippie idealism, so the "Brummie Beatles" stamped on the petals of flower power. For the band, a textbook career of madness, mayhem and multimillion album sales ensued. And it was all thanks to horror films and one demonic vision. Nothing more gothic than that.

The band had been happily labouring under the name Earth until another band claimed the moniker was theirs. As they stood outside their rehearsal room wondering what to call themselves now, bassist and lyricist Geezer Butler saw a long queue outside the cinema opposite, waiting to see the 1964 Boris Karloff film *Black Sabbath*. "Strange," pondered Butler, "that people spend so much money to see scary movies." Inspiration fixed, he and Osbourne wrote a song of the same name, using the writings of Dennis Wheatley as their muse.

Butler declared he was sparked to write the words by waking up one night to see a shadowy silhouetted figure standing at the foot of his bed. The band's music matched, if not subtly, his sense of the eerie. Creepy imagery was given gearshifts and gravitas by innovative guitarist Tony Iommi's use of unorthodox tunings and a musical tritone, commonly known as "the Devil's interval". Black Sabbath therefore didn't sound like every other hard-rockin', no-nonsense riffin', bunch of longhaired blokes in jeans. Their music loomed as well as boomed – ominously, portentously – making the lyrics and Ozzy's borderline-ridiculous, helium-high, nasal vocals unsettling rather than risible.

Recorded in one day (all first takes), the album made number eight in the UK but kicked off a surprisingly enduring legend. It was "so influential", said *Q* magazine, "that it remains a template for metal bands many decades on." And not just metal bands. Various critics have cited The Sabbs as pioneers of doom rock, stoner rock and, yes, Goth. "We just played our live set and that was it," Iommi shrugged. "We actually thought a whole day [to record] was quite a long time." Butler has protested that the track "N.I.B" was actually about Satan falling in love and becoming a "good" person, and "The Wizard" was, like so many songs of the period, inspired by the books of J.R.R. Tolkien.

The sleeve featured a black-clad woman standing in front of a watermill. It was shot at Mapledurham, a village on the Thames in Oxfordshire. Unclear, unexplained, the image is as sinister as sinister gets. Who was this woman? Iommi has forgotten her name, but says she turned up backstage at one of the

OPPOSITE

Black Sabbath in concert at The Paradiso, Amsterdam, in 1971. The band took its name from the 1964 Boris Karloff film.

band's early shows and introduced herself. She remains an enigmatic icon of gothic-related music. The album's original gatefold sleeve showed, on the inside, an inverted cross and a poem. Not that the band knew about it until later; some members were already aghast that the press was describing them as satanists or occultists. For America, the inner-sleeve idea was vetoed.

Indeed, in the States, Black Sabbath were not instantly embraced. "Bullshit necromancy," roared *The Village Voice*, "the worst of the counter-culture." High-profile critic Lester Bangs said the inane lyrics paid tribute to Aleister Crowley. So much for reviews, the album became a fixture on the *Billboard* charts for over a year, and a portal to the peculiar 1970s. The Sabbs' decade began with the band recording their follow-up, *Paranoid* – their first British number one album, and their last until 2013. *Paranoid* sold 12 million copies worldwide, so venturing into the dark side wasn't commercial suicide. People had subliminal cravings, and Sabbath's nocturnal numbskull shrieks satisfied something previously unspoken.

Ozzy, of course, went on to become, with his spooky-ooky-ooky family, an unlikely reality-TV star and "treasured institution", but not before years of mock-satanic behaviour. A clown, rather than a dark prince, perhaps, but one with tears: drink and drugs have led to severe illness. In 2013, he admitted he was once again "in a very dark place". Yet he survives, with Black Sabbath's rapturously received comeback album *13*, their first studio album with Ozzy in three and a half decades, featuring song titles like "Is God Dead?" and "The End of the Beginning". Of its difficult birth, Geezer Butler said, "Sometimes it felt like there was a curse on us." When the band was given a major award as a "living legend", Ozzy muttered, "That's better than being a dead one."

The Heart of Illumination

"I don't think I'm responsible for anything," snapped the notoriously surly Lou Reed in 1977. The Velvet Underground, however, reign undisputed as one of history's most influential rock and roll bands. Their radical reinventions of sound and literacy probed a heart of darkness from which The Beatles and The Stones, for all their flickers of pioneering spirit, shied away. They have come to symbolize New York's artier leanings in the mid- to late 1960s sly, sleazy-sweet "kinky" aura annexed to Andy Warhol's much-mythologized Factory scene.

Warhol saw something shadowy in them. Was it gothic? Certainly the taboos and themes covered by Reed's lyrics and John Cale's experimentation hit upon a then-new counter-cultural charisma. Reed said, "Andy told me that what we were doing with music was the same thing he was doing with painting and movies – i.e. not kidding around. It was very, very real… not slick or a lie." If this in itself didn't constitute "gothic", the addition to the ranks of former model-actress Nico, with her stentorian voice and sombre presence, brooked no argument. She was the gothic incarnate. Born in Germany to Spanish/Yugoslav parents, the enigmatic blonde had already turned down a film contract with Federico Fellini (although she can be seen in *La Dolce Vita*). Warhol's mixed-media event *Uptight*, with strobes and spotlights and writhing dancers and the screeching feedback of The Velvets in their sunglasses, coalesced as *Exploding Plastic Inevitable*, and it got New York buzzing. "Grotesque," ran one report. "Revolutionary," said Warhol. "Fun," said Reed. It paid for The Velvet's 1967, banana-sleeve-sporting debut album, the diplomatically titled *The Velvet Underground and Nico*. It gave the world songs such as "All Tomorrow's Parties", "Venus in Furs", "Heroin", "Sunday Morning" and "Waiting for the Man" (later performed by Bauhaus on the B-side of "Bela Lugosi's Dead"). With its sneers and shudders and risqué language, it stands as one of the templates of gothic music, a licentious, unsettling landmark.

Their second album, *White Light/White Heat* (1968), also mapped out new milieus. The Velvet Underground were rock and roll's original creatures of the night. "If it wasn't me," remarked Reed, "I would have idolized myself in The Velvets. I loved what we did… we stood for everything kids loved and adults hated. We were loud, we were vulgar, we sang about dope, sex, violence, you name it." As he did so often, Reed contradicted the received wisdoms. "But it wasn't the 'nocturnal' side of rock and roll – it was the daylight side. No one else had noticed it, that's all. We didn't know why everyone was reeling in shock."

BELOW

Warhol famously designed the album sleeve for The Velvet Underground and Nico, *released in March 1967.*

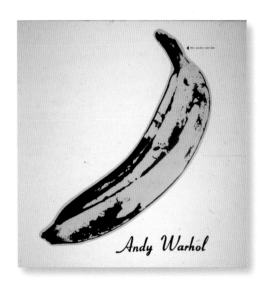

When The Velvets ran aground on personality clashes and ego/control issues, Reed went on to a solo career, which burst into glam-pop life with the Bowie-assisted album *Transformer* and "Walk on the Wild Side". He reacted badly to fame and perhaps overcompensated by making "difficult" and diverse (though never less than fascinating) records through the 1970s. Among the albums (close to 30) that he made up until his death in 2013, there are several that shiver with the spirit of the gothic: the perverse *Metal Machine Music*, the noir narratives of *Street Hassle* and *The Bells*, the Poe-inspired *The Raven*, the investigations of mortality that are *Songs for Drella* (with John Cale) and *Magic and Loss*. His gothic masterpiece, however, is 1973's monumental and macabre *Berlin*, which regularly tops any smirking list of "The Most Depressing Albums of All Time".

It drew alarming vitriol and bile from critics, who'd expected a sensible career move after "Walk on the Wild Side". Yet to his newer audience of teenage fans it sounded epic, stunning and stirring; as music producer Bob Ezrin put it, "a film for the ears". Ezrin was young, ambitious and fearless, high on his recent successes with Alice Cooper (no stranger to the darker elements of performance),

"We didn't know why everyone was reeling in shock," shrugged Lou Reed in response to comments about The Velvet Underground's music. The band are pictured here with mentor Andy Warhol (centre). Nico is bottom left.

and would go on to help build Pink Floyd's own neo-gothic cry for help, *The Wall*. Constructing *Berlin*, both Reed and Ezrin pushed themselves close to nervous breakdown. When it was finished, Ezrin suggested to the singer that, "the best idea is we put it in a box, put the box in a closet, leave it there and never listen to it again". It was an exorcism of sorts, utterly uncompromising in its starkness and candour, genuinely chilling to hear. "We killed ourselves psychologically on that record," said Reed. "We went so far into it that it was kind of hard to get out." Loosely the story of a doomed, needy ménage à trois in the titular anxiety-riddled city, it covered obsessive jealousy, domestic violence, drugs, comedowns, bad parenting and suicide. Over the baroque, rock-operatic music, Reed's monotone, apathetic, ennui-laden voice just added to the sense of angst. "It's involved with violence," he explained, "both mental and physical. The important thing is the relationship between the characters. The narrator is filling you in from his point of view, and his point of view is not particularly pleasant."

Some claim that Reed's own crumbling marriage to Bettye, who attempted suicide shortly afterwards, was the source material. Others believe Nico was the muse, although, according to Reed, "She didn't understand a word of it." Either way, *Berlin*, climaxing after babies crying and wrist-cutting with "Sad Song", was a film for the ears with "no happy ending". The outraged reviews broke Reed's heart, perhaps going some way to explaining his increased stroppiness with journalists from then on. "The way that album was overlooked was probably the biggest disappointment I ever faced. I pulled the blinds down shut at that point… and they've remained closed."

Reed's last recorded work, the poorly received *Lulu* collaboration with Metallica, proved he never lost his will to write about harrowing, confrontational subjects (sex, abuse, Jack the Ripper). I asked him what kept drawing him back to the heart of darkness. "I wouldn't call it the heart of darkness," he replied. "I'd call it the heart of illumination. It's not a party record. The mind is the most erogenous zone I know. This is where I like to exist." Anyone intrigued by what we call the gothic will empathize with that.

ABOVE

Reed performing in Copenhagen in August 1973, with guitarist Dick Wagner.

BELOW

Berlin (1973) was Lou Reed's darkest album: a "film for the ears" with "no happy ending".

Don't Turn on the Light

Leonard Cohen sang on his debut album *Songs of Leonard Cohen* (1967): "O the sisters of mercy they are not departed or gone / They were waiting for me when I thought that I just can't go on." When Leeds boys Andrew Eldritch and Gary Marx heard the song in the Robert Altman film *McCabe & Mrs. Miller*, they found a name for their nascent group. The Sisters of Mercy were to become one of the great Goth bands. Cohen, of course, has achieved a whole lot more besides since then.

The resignation and amplified despair in Cohen's love-it-or-hate-it voice, his wry, often-under-appreciated humour, his fatalism and fascination with art and sex – all these mark him as a proto-Goth, if you will. *Songs of Leonard Cohen* is a testament to ennui and exasperation, frustration and disappointment. Montreal-born Leonard wasn't making it as a poet or a novelist, although his novel *Beautiful Losers* has a great gothic title. His idea of a fall-back strategy was to move to New York and become a confessional singer-songwriter. There, he fell in unrequited love with Nico.

The 33-year-old newcomer was soon acclaimed as the bard of romantic outsiders. By 1988 and the mock-jaunty *I'm Your Man* album, he was singing "I ache in the places I used to play." Nobody's claiming he sang about vampires per se (at least not above the subtext), but if Cohen, still touring at a venerable age to increasingly vast rapt audiences, wasn't an influence on the tone and stance and attitude of Goth, nobody was. The song "Sisters of Mercy" went on: "When I left they were sleeping, I hope you run into them soon / Don't turn on the light, you can read their address by the moon."

ABOVE
Montreal's mock-morose "godfather of gloom", Leonard Cohen, in Amsterdam, 1972.

Dead Babies

There is much that's truly gothic in the beautiful bruised ballads of Scott Walker's first four solo albums: try "Montagu Terrace (In Blue)" from *Scott*, or "Duchess" from *Scott 4*, and in Phil Spector's ambi-emotional Wall of Sound creations. More flamboyantly, no discussion of gothic music would be complete without a spotlight on Alice Cooper, "the godfather of shock rock". In parts closer to high farce than worrisome art statement, sure, but his horror-show antics certainly unnerved the defenders of all that is correct and "normal".

Alice, real name Vincent Damon Furnier, was born in 1948, the son of a preacher man. His stage shows have involved electric chairs, guillotines, boa constrictors and decapitated dolls. His 1973 tour boasted an inventory that included "a dentist's chair, four hundred pints of fake blood, twenty-three thousand sparklers, mannequins, costumes…" A confused, illicit thrill ran through rock fans when his band's breakthrough hit "School's Out" rang bells in summer 1972.

Alice has drawn inspiration from both horror movies and vaudeville. He cited Screamin' Jay Hawkins as a forefather for his macabre stage props. At the time, the sexual androgyny of his name drew more criticism than his nightly mock executions. "We were into fun, sex, death and money when everybody was into peace and love," he noted. "We wanted to see what was next. It turned out we were next, and we drove a stake through the heart of the Love Generation."

He, too, worked with Bob Ezrin, and Alice's tongue-in-cheek controversy – a precursor to Marilyn Manson's persona and career in many ways – flirted with grotesque imagery onstage and on album, dropping in titles like "Sick Things", "I Love the Dead", "Welcome to My Nightmare" and "Dead Babies".

Vince was and is, in reality, a golf-playing, restaurant-owning, born-again Christian, and an articulate guy who is keenly aware of the absurdity of his alter ego's showbiz posturing, though he has gone through times of wrestling with real demons, such as drink and drugs. His ability to be both professionally loathsome and personally lovable has seen him exchange dialogues with everyone from artist Salvador Dalí to politician David Blunkett. His 2007 autobiography bore the title *Alice Cooper, Golf Monster*. By 2012, he was a cherished gothic institution like Ozzy Osbourne and starring as himself in Tim Burton's *Dark Shadows*. Johnny Depp's character remarked that he was the ugliest woman he'd ever seen.

OPPOSITE
Snakes alive! Shock'n'roller Alice Cooper on stage in the early 1970s.

BELOW
With his trademark black eye make-up, Alice Cooper drew inspiration from horror films as well as vaudeville for his stage performances.

Nightclubbing

Emanating from David Bowie's significant Berlin period, Iggy Pop's 1977 debut solo album *The Idiot* (co-written and produced by Bowie) has been cited by some as a seminal "gothic" work. In truth, this distinctive piece pretty much invents its own genre, one that Bowie further explored on his landmark *Low* and *Heroes* masterpieces of the same era. (*Low* was released before *The Idiot*, but the pair had begun work on Iggy's album first, with Bowie perhaps using it as a testing ground for ideas.)

OPPOSITE

Calling Sister Midnight: the inimitable Iggy Pop at London's Rainbow Theatre on The Idiot *tour of 1977.*

With his previous band The Stooges, Iggy, like Alice, like The Velvet Underground, could be said to have stomped on the peace-and-love generation. *The Idiot*, inspired by the Dostoevsky novel, is a dark psychological journey of sound and words, introspective but futuristic. "A funky, robotic hellhole of an album," wrote Bowie biographer David Buckley. Iggy used Oedipal dream imagery, Bowie urging him on to write about "walking through the night like ghosts". "China Girl", which was later performed by Bowie, was a candid love song full of daring couplets (swastikas, sacred cows), while the charmingly jaded "Funtime" (also covered by Peter Murphy) and the theatrical "Dum Dum Boys" both qualify as proto-gothic, pre-dating the British post-punk, which mutated into "Goth". *Rolling Stone* reckoned, somewhat unfortunately, that *The Idiot* was "a necrophiliac's delight".

Siouxsie Sioux, who covered the track "Nightclubbing" with The Creatures, hailed the album as an inspiration, while Depeche Mode and Nine Inch Nails clocked its highly original electronic-industrial elements. The latter's Trent Reznor sampled "Nightclubbing" for his 1994 hit "Closer". Clearly, anything to do with the flamboyant ennui of Bowie (there had been grand gothic gestures on the *Diamond Dogs* album) was a major spark for Bauhaus and others. And the place of *The Idiot* in the evolution and mythology of gothic music was confirmed, poignantly, when, in 1980, it was found still playing on Joy Division singer Ian Curtis' turntable after he'd hanged himself. It is indisputably an otherworldly record.

ABOVE

Nine Inch Nails, led by Trent Reznor, in 1994: Reznor sampled Iggy's "Nightclubbing" for his hit "Closer".

Closer

If Siouxsie and the Banshees were born in the visceral punk era before blossoming, Joy Division and The Cure emerged from the artier, book-reading environs of post-punk. Both can lay claim to having spawned Goth, though fans of both would counter that there was more to them than that. Joy Division's initial success engendered a devout following, initially around Manchester, of "intense young men dressed in grey overcoats", labelled the "Cult with No Name". The overcoats persisted among audiences of Echo & The Bunnymen, The Sound and Comsat Angels, even early U2, but felt like a symbol of a separate strain to the more midnight-black trappings of Goth. What Joy Division definitely had that filtered into Goth was an air of doomed melancholy, with sadness, furrowed brows and troubled psyches replacing the spit, rage and clenched fists of punk.

Joy Division were the first band described as "gothic" by commentators of the period. Their clammy-rain atmosphere, their use of high bass lines (by Peter Hook) tackling melodic roles and, of course, Ian Curtis' stentorian/pseudo-operatic low voice were to influence the leaders of the Goth pack and, decades on, revivalists like Interpol and Editors. Bono of U2 wrote in 2006: "It would be hard to find a darker place in music than Joy Division. Their name, their lyrics, and their singer were as big a black cloud as you could find in the sky." He went on to call their work a search for truth and beauty, and there is something in that: for all the nocturnal surfaces of Goth, its highpoints represent a quest for the release of euphoria. To "break on through to the other side", as Ian Curtis favourites The Doors had phrased it.

Unknown Pleasures and *Closer*, the band's two albums made before Curtis' death, were the John the Baptist of Goth. After Curtis committed suicide on May 18, 1980, *NME*'s Charles Shaar Murray, reviewing *Closer* in July, remarked that "it would be demeaning to all concerned… to treat *Closer* as some sort of elaborate suicide note, dissect the lines and words for evidence of chronic depression…" And yet, he added, "If Joy Division did anything, it was to centre their music around a refusal to pretend that everything was all right… *Closer* is, in the most strict and literal sense of the term… a matter of life and death." "Love Will Tear Us Apart" was inscribed by Curtis' widow on his memorial stone.

OPPOSITE
The late Ian Curtis of Joy Division, claimed by many to be the first band referred to as "gothic".

BELOW
Joy Division's Closer: *"a matter of life and death".*

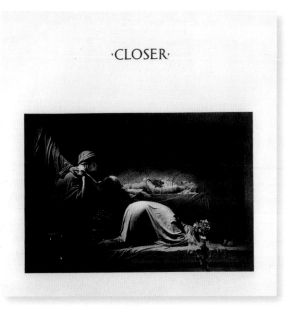

·CLOSER·

The Head on the Door

By the 1990s, The Cure had become one of the biggest "alternative" rock bands on the planet. And they had got there by playing tormented, turbulent music (as represented on early albums like *Faith* and *Pornography*)… at least until lead singer Robert Smith decided, early in the 1980s, that he was fed up with their "gloomy" reputation.

While their albums continued to deal with paranoia and unease, he added a little pop spice to their murky brew, creating wryly energetic hits like "Love Cats", "Just Like Heaven" and "Friday I'm In Love". Somehow The Cure became the most keenly loved of Goth bands, as well as a hugely successful commercial beast, playful and crowd-pleasing, and subsequently a primary influence on Interpol, Smashing Pumpkins and many more.

The gothic tag from which they cringed had been set in stone by nihilistic lyrics and intense extended workouts like "A Forest". One member left after their first world tour, claiming, "I realized that the group was heading towards suicidal, sombre music… that didn't interest me at all." Smith was so engrossed in the early sounds that he would leave the stage in tears. He was "undergoing a lot of mental stress", he admitted. "It had nothing to do with the group, just… what I was like, my age. I was a pretty monstrous sort of person at that time." Bassist Simon Gallup added, "Nihilism took over. We'd sing, 'it doesn't matter if we all die', and that is exactly what we thought at the time." The *Faith* album – tracks include "The Funeral Party", "The Drowning Man", "The Holy Hour" and "All Cats Are Grey" – is a Goth landmark, bringing in references to Camus, Tennyson and a girl named Fuchsia. "One day I'd wake up wanting to kill somebody, the next I wouldn't even bother getting up," Smith told music journalist Paul Morley. "I was shutting down."

Yet as The Cure lightened up over the 1980s, journalists meeting them would find beer in full flow and Smith as likely to talk about QPR football club as anything "doomy". *The Head on the Door* (1985) was "a collection of pop songs… bursting with hits". In *Melody Maker*, I reviewed 1987's *Kiss Me Kiss Me Kiss Me* as "tortured memories and current fun". I interviewed Smith in Brussels that December. There was much drinking among the band, who couldn't leave their hotel for fear of being mobbed, while they watched the film *Koyaanisqatsi* and old "Dr Who" videos. "I'm seen as being cuddly, and my mouth and lipstick are supposed to be so nice," protested Robert. "This isn't true; I'm as horrible as anyone." He added, "I'm wearing black for the first time in years today. We wear white on stage. We look like angels." He admitted to writing lyrics inspired by Baudelaire, Rimbaud and Verlaine. And Sartre. Did he ever forget himself, lose himself? "Yeah, after about the seventeenth Guinness. Late night swimming in dark waters is good too. And sleep!"

"Most people's devil is far more pronounced than their angel," he continued. "I think the angel probably visits, while the devil lives here. Although I'm turning around a bit: I'm losing my cynicism as I get older!" Did he recognize the labels people gave him, such as the Messiah of Angst? "I never thought those descriptions referred to me. I didn't go home and find my mum saying, 'Hello, Messiah of Angst, welcome home!'" So when I read these things I either laugh or just go, 'Oh, nutty bastards'. How could I stay as one thing for years anyway? Back then, I'd feel… overwhelming despair or deliriously happy. Now I'm not shocked anymore. Some days, especially on tour, you just know nothing's going to happen. Nothing's to be felt. It's another day gone." I ask him: is it worth being alive on those days? He looks up, with a puzzled expression. "No… not really."

In 1989 Smith was stating that the new album *Disintegration* wasn't miserable "at all". I reviewed it as "about as much fun as losing a limb… challenging, claustrophobic" (I liked it). His first line on the record was, "I think it's dark and looks like rain." His last? "I'll never lose this pain." This, too, from my review: "The words which (spring to mind)… are words now devalued and used only to mock Goths: doom, gloom, barren, despair…"

ABOVE
"I'll never lose this pain," sang The Cure's anguished Robert Smith, but perhaps not while reading The Beano *in bed in New York in 1986.*

Undead, Undead, Undead

Such words were used again and again in the golden age of Goth, but it was resilient. By the time the Goth greats of the 1980s picked up the torch from the pioneers of earlier decades, the unspoken had become more articulate. Artful. Aware of its aesthetic. Loquacious, even. Peter Murphy, frontman of Bauhaus, knew that the visual mattered as much as the sonic.

Murphy, over a cappuccino, monologues about his solo work, Marilyn Manson ("a Munsters version of something that was once pure and new and British") and the thin line between genius and autism. (This was before he got arrested in Los Angeles, in 2013, for driving under the influence, hit-and-run driving, and methamphetamine possession. He was sentenced to three years' probation.)

Of Bauhaus, the band with which he made his name, he said, "We were termed 'gothic as a brick' by one paper. This was 1981, when the press either built you up or killed you, so I almost believed it. But look at it now – we were minimalist, never used colours, yet were theatrical and artistic, in a raw way. We were very, very alternative. I was a bastard Nijinsky. We were the antithesis of everything that was fashionable then: all that screaming-about-nothing protest that was punk. They were flailing

OPPOSITE
"We were original. We were glam. And we were beautiful": Bauhaus, 1982.

LEFT
"The bats have left the bell tower…" – Bauhaus made their name with *"Bela Lugosi's Dead".*

to find something to scream about, and ran out after five minutes. We were original. We were glam. And we were beautiful."

Formed in Northampton in 1978, Bauhaus kicked against the pricks and swiftly rose to heroic levels of cult-dom and were labelled by many as the first "gothic rock" or "Goth" band. "It's undeniable there was a gothic element there," says ex-guitarist David J. "We did have a fascination with the darkly romantic. But there were so many other sides to the band, so the term became somewhat limiting: sometimes we'd go purposely against what was expected of us in that regard, which was a lot of fun. See? We had *'fun'*!" His younger brother, drummer Kevin Haskins, says, "Yes, we chose to wear black and our first single was about a vampire and our music for the most part was dark. But we didn't feel we belonged in that or any other movement…"

Bauhaus blazed briefly, splitting in 1983. There were subsequent reformations. Yet their work here was, effectively, done. For at least one generation, they had invented "Goth". After just six weeks together, they'd released their debut single "Bela Lugosi's Dead" – nine minutes of hypnotic horror-lyrics and trippy dub, which took up residence on the indie charts for two years. It may have meant they were the butt of Count Dracula jokes for the rest of their career, but even now it's an alarmingly brilliant first record, sounding like little else above ground. "We were elated and excited that we were capable of conjuring forth such a beautiful monster!" says David. "I remember having chills running up my spine," recalls Kevin. "We all knew that we'd recorded something very special."

David J had chosen the band name (originally "Bauhaus 1919") after the German art movement. "It occurred to me that our sound, and to a degree our aesthetic, was stark and stripped-down. Everything was honed so as to exclude excess. Which is ironic, as that's the *opposite* of 'gothic'." Like most bands who defined the classic British "Goth" era, they deny being "Goth". This is a recurring theme. Post-punk? Alternative 1980s? Fine. But few of them actively want to be remembered as "Goth", a term they feel was tarnished by late-arrivals who jumped on the bandwagon and made the movement a subject of much ribbing.

The most defining, narcissistically joyous Bauhaus moment on film is the opening sequence of Tony Scott's 1983 film *The Hunger*. As vampires Catherine Deneuve and David Bowie lure unsuspecting victims to an evening of filthy sex and gory bloodshed, "Bela Lugosi's Dead" plays stealthily over the narrative, while a spooky, razor-cheekboned, stellar-looking Murphy (also a model) writhes, lip-syncs and throws convincing shapes to camera. It's not just a great Bauhaus moment, it's a great moment in the history of arthouse-highbrow-porn-chiller cinema – the band stealing the scene from their own hero, Ziggy Stardust.

"I was the apex of the triangle," reflects Murphy. "The body of the pyramid is the band and the music, but at the front you're what it all comes out of. And it wasn't flagrant ego: it was smarter, more artistic, more erotic."

Peter Murphy during Bauhaus' "Ziggy Stardust" video shoot at the Roundhouse, London. "I was the apex of the triangle," he said.

Spellbound

OPPOSITE

On stage in signature gothic gear, Siouxsie and the Banshees (with Robert Smith on guitar), 1984. Despite appearances, guitarist John McGeoch claimed that the band was "more thriller than horror movie".

Speaking of Siouxsie and the Banshees' 1981 album *Juju* (their fourth), Siouxsie Sioux mused, "I've always thought that one of our greatest strengths was our ability to craft tension in music and subject matter.

"*Juju* had a strong identity, which the Goth bands that came in our wake tried to mimic, but they simply ended up diluting it. They were using horror as the basis for stupid rock'n'roll pantomime. There was no sense of tension in their music." That the Banshees were ever a Goth band was "simply not true", insisted guitarist John McGeoch. "It simplifies things too much to give it a label like that. We were more thriller than horror movie, more Hitchcockian blood dripping on a daisy than putting fangs in something." "Voodoo Dolly", which became a live-set closer, was "the song which brought all the fans' skulls and beads out," bassist Steven Severin said. "But if *Juju* had a horror theme to it, it was psychological; nothing to do with ghosts and ghouls."

Having emerged during punk with *The Scream* (and catching the eye of British TV presenter Bill Grundy), then bringing the avant-garde into post-punk on *Kaleidoscope*, the band always refuted the Goth tag, but Siouxsie and her sidekicks' visual image was much siphoned by the genre. Siouxsie's spiky black hair and fetish-bondage-influenced clothes, cat-eye make-up and ruby-red lipstick became signature glam Goth-wear. The group's subsequent albums of the 1980s – *A Kiss in the Dreamhouse*, *Hyaena*, *Tinderbox* and *Peepshow* – undeniably flirted with sinister, twisted fairy-tale imagery. Robert Smith of The Cure even joined the band between 1982 and 1984, after McGeoch was fired for drink problems. As late as 1995, their final album *The Rapture* (co-produced by The Velvet Underground's John Cale) was described by *Melody Maker* as "a fascinating journey through danger and exotica".

The influential *Juju*, with such challenging and provocative hits as "Spellbound" and "Arabian Knights", stands as perhaps the band's definitive "gothic" masterpiece: it bewitched and bewildered, proving the Banshees were more than just another bunch of punk chancers and establishing them long-term as serious, transgressive artists. Steven Severin and McGeoch claimed they'd wanted to emulate the feel of *Their Satanic Majesties Request* by The Rolling Stones, though it came out chillier, more crooked than that. Betty Page of *Sounds* wrote, "This is the soundtrack of the unknown, hinting darkly at black magic, witchery, murder and death."

As "Night Shift" nodded to the Yorkshire Ripper, "Head Cut" served up imagery concerning severed and shrunken heads, and "Halloween" saw Siouxsie chanting "trick or treat", there can be little doubt that *Juju* – half fireworks, half icy hauteur – is one of the great, nocturnal Goth templates. Spellbound, for sure. It sends you spinning. You have no choice.

RIGHT

"I know what's best. That's my job, and my brief – to do what I want." Andrew Eldritch of The Sisters of Mercy, at Wembley Arena, London, 1990.

Murky Depths

Andrew Eldritch gave great interviews. Smart, laconic, erudite, sarcastic, candid, caustic, deluded but somehow not deluded, this cat-loving reluctant frontman made The Sisters of Mercy even more entertaining than their overt image as gloomy Horsemen of the Apocalypse ascending enigmatically on a black cloud over Hades. "I've always taken the view that what I want to give them is what they need," the self-proclaimed Elvis-meets-Kierkegaard told me in 1990. "What they want is neither here nor there. I know what's best. That's my job, and my brief. To do what I want." Is that the role of the rock star? "It's the role of a great one. Particularly in a medium as wonderfully ludicrous as rock'n'roll." He pulled the plug in 1993 in protest against record company Time Warner and hasn't released a record since. "I don't have the existential need to do so. I'm not much of an extrovert."

First and Last and Always (1985) was mostly spawned of music by Wayne Hussey and words by Eldritch. "Black Planet", "No Time To Cry" and the title track are pinnacles of Goth. Hussey and Craig Adams, alienated by Eldritch, promptly left, forming The Sisterhood, named after the band's fan community. Eldritch protested; later, Hussey admitted, "I think Andrew was right… it was a bit cheap." His band took the name The Mission, who also survived as stalwarts of the Goth era. Eldritch signed up the exceedingly Goth-looking bassist Patricia Morrison (formerly of The Gun Club), who wound up playing more of a part in promo photos and videos than on tracks, and then recorded with Meat Loaf co-writer Jim Steinman, delivering the *Floodland* album (1987) and the epic lead single "This Corrosion". "It's ridiculous," he told music journalist Paul Elliott. "It's supposed to be ridiculous. It's a song about ridiculousness. I told Steinman we needed something that sounded like a disco party run by the Borgias. And that's what we got." "Lucretia My Reflection", also on the album, is one of the all-time arch moments of Goth.

The third Sisters' line-up saw Eldritch roping in Tony James (ex Sigue Sigue Sputnik and Generation X), Tim Bricheno (once of All about Eve, another much-loved band of the era, fronted by singer Julianne Regan) and German guitarist Andreas Bruhn. The heavy-rock album *Vision Thing* (1990) lampooned American politics. "*Floodland* has got an awful lot of murky depths, and that's fine, but I wanted less of the murk on *Vision Thing*." The Sisters soared relatively briefly but brilliantly, capable even of wooing a Goth-packed, dry-ice-filled Royal Albert Hall with a cover of Hot Chocolate's classic death-ballad "Emma". Eldritch now says being in the public eye makes him "uncomfortable", but his contribution to the gothic is deathless. Asked recently what the biggest myth about him is, he replied, "People think that I live in a Bavarian castle surrounded by bats." In fact, he said, he prefers to "watch suspect Japanese films and listen to cricket all day".

"I hear the roar of a big machine/Two worlds and in between"

"Lucretia My Reflection" by The Sisters of Mercy

BELOW
The 1988 Floodland *incarnation of The Sisters of Mercy: Patricia Morrison and Andrew Eldritch.*

Tender Prey

Were there limitless space, I'd eulogize at length here about The Mission, Fields of the Nephilim, All About Eve and German art-niks Xmal Deutschland (whose *Fetisch* and *Tocsin* albums are gloriously gothic, fiercely elegant). Cocteau Twins, Dead Can Dance and a myriad other 4AD acts, not least co-founder Ivo Watts-Russell's This Mortal Coil project (see, especially, *Filigree and Shadow*) ooze gothic flavour, though probably transcended the genre. Many might posit The Cramps. No discussion of the gothic is complete without reiterating the enduring efforts of Nick Cave & The Bad Seeds, to this day singing of death and doom and consumptive passion with a knowing wink. On Cave's acclaimed 2013 album *Push the Sky Away*, the centrepiece track "Higgs Boson Blues" sees the Australian (after referencing Robert Johnson) crying, "Well, here comes Lucifer, with his canon law / And a hundred black babies running from his homicidal jaw…"

Reviewing Cave's 1988 album *Tender Prey* in *Melody Maker*, I cited "The Mercy Seat" as "demonic and devout… as near to humming the executioner's song as anyone will ever get". The same year, All About Eve's Julianne Regan explained to me her love of the classic gothic film *La Belle et La Bête*. "I'm a sucker for romance, so I want the beauty to love the beast. Then when he turns into a handsome prince at the end, I'm disappointed: I prefer him as the beast because he's more hopeless. It's too happy an ending."

They also served the beautiful beast, either in the front line or tangentially: Crime & The City Solution, The Cult, The Damned, Gary Numan, Specimen, Clan of Xymox, Killing Joke, Gene Loves Jezebel, Alien Sex Fiend, Danielle Dax, Flesh for Lulu, The March Violets, Skeletal Family, The Rose of Avalanche, Inca Babies, The Gun Club, Ministry, Laibach, White Zombie, Machines of Loving Grace, Paradise Lost, Coil, Evanescence, Interpol.

As The Mission and Fields of the Nephilim launched a co-headline tour in the winter of 2013/14, the latter's leader Carl McCoy told *Classic Rock* magazine, "When we started, the whole 'Goth' tag didn't exist. Goth meant architecture to me. The whole 'goth rock' thing started in the late 1980s, but in fact it's the fans who are categorized as 'Goths'."

And, lest we forget, the heyday of Echo & The Bunnymen, The Sound and Comsat Angels saw the grandeur and brooding of the gothic surging through albums like *Ocean Rain*, *From the Lion's Mouth* and *Waiting for a Miracle*. Sidestep into more electronica-based sounds, and you discern the same strains pulsing through Japan's *Gentlemen Take Polaroids*, Soft Cell's *The Art of Falling Apart* and *This Last Night in Sodom* and Depeche Mode's more introspective moments, and overtly glowing on Propaganda's Poe-inspired "A Dream within a Dream" and "Dr. Mabuse". Yet, as we advised earlier, gothic music was not just confined to 1980s "Goth" and its spin-offs. It persists relentlessly.

*Anja Huwe of
underrated and
uncompromising
German band Xmal
Deutschland, live at
Brixton, London,
1984.*

LEFT

*Nick Cave has
carved out a durable
career with tales of
death, doom and
desire.*

OPPOSITE

The Cult fused "the pseudo-mysticism of The Doors" with "touches of post-punk goth-rock".

ABOVE

Songs the Lord Taught Us: The Cramps, featuring Lux Interior and Poison Ivy, in 1986.

NEXT PAGE

If I Was Your Vampire: Marilyn Manson rebooted goth for the 1990s.

Antichrist Superstars

Of all the latter-day unholy saints of "industrial Goth" bearing the torch, Marilyn Manson towers: a controversial, commercially successful titan. His album titles include *Antichrist Superstar, Smells Like Children, The Golden Age of Grotesque* and *Born Villain*. He knows what he's doing, does Brian Warner. Of his sixth album *Eat Me, Drink Me*, he offered, "I'd say it's got a cannibal, consumptive, obsessive, violent-sex, romance angle. But with an upbeat swing to it." Its opening track "If I Was Your Vampire" crystallizes his shock-rock career, sounding like Bauhaus on steroids, singing with irony: "blood-stained sheets in the shape of your heart" and "everything's black / no turning back". When scapegoated for the Columbine shootings in 1999 because the killers were purported fans, he said, "Blaming me was ridiculous. If you want to blame something, well, I went to a Christian school. That's why I write what I write. Shall we blame the Christians?"

When Manson toured with Alice Cooper last year, the elder statesman said, "We have a lot in common in that we both play and created monster characters. How do you deal with that against your real life? I've had a lot more time with Alice, so I know when to be Alice and when not to be Alice. I told Marilyn it's very hard to maintain a character 24 hours a day. I once thought I had to be that character all the time – and it nearly killed me. But he's very smart, he's got good insight. I can at least show him and Rob Zombie where the thin ice is."

Trent Reznor of Nine Inch Nails, whose industrial-rock project album *Pretty Hate Machine* (1989) became another modern gothic landmark, chose to record its follow-up *The Downward Spiral* in the mansion where the Charles Manson murders took place in 1969. Reznor claims to have played Bowie's *Low* constantly for inspiration there. Lately, he's cleaned up his act and admitted, very un-Gothly, to being "pretty happy".

Finnish band HIM's (His Infernal Majesty) lead singer Ville Valo is the gothic-rock pin-up of recent years. The band's first EP was called *666 Ways to Love*; their first album *Greatest Lovesongs Vol. 666*. Fans of The Sisters of Mercy, Black Sabbath and Fields of the Nephilim, HIM emphasize that any references to Satan are "symbolic – regarding the darker side of love". Valo says, "I think we are a special shade of Goth, more tender than the others. Very melancholic." That said, their Beelzebub-baiting debut included hidden tracks numbered 10–66, which filled 666 megabytes but were silent, bar track 66, bringing the album's official length to 66 minutes and 6 seconds.

*LA band 45 Grave – and singer Dinah
Cancer – formed in 1979 and were
progenitors of horror punk. 2012 saw their
first new album in 27 years.*

ABOVE

*Finnish band HIM (His Infernal Majesty)
debuted with an EP called 666 Ways to
Love. "I think we are a special shade of
Goth," says lead singer Ville Valo.*

"I like to pose the question to myself: Am I a man who thinks he's an Angel, or an Angel who thinks he's a man?"

Marilyn Manson

Dead Nature

In 2014, the gothic still does not sleep. Today there is something of the gothic in the music of Savages, PJ Harvey, The Horrors and Anna Calvi. Musicians may cringe at the label of "post-gothic", but the attitude, the mannerisms, twitch ever on. Listen closely and you can hear twinkling re-imaginings and reference points nestling half-hidden among the output of Placebo, Queens of the Stone Age, Vampire Weekend, Zola Jesus. Cult artist Steven Wilson's *The Raven That Refused to Sing (And Other Stories)* is rich with pulses of Poe. Ones-to-watch like Nadine Shah, Bethia Beadman, Dum Dum Girls and The Gaslight Troubadours keep the flame alive, consciously or unconsciously. If Lady Gaga's music is knowingly trashy dance-pop, her persona and videos (and her Little Monsters fanbase) often embrace gothic imagery. Meanwhile, hauntology, a singularly unsettling "genre", is given showcase nights in highbrow arts venues.

The gothic in music endures and resurrects itself, immortal, an undead ringer for love. A heart of simmering darkness. A blinding, brilliant light.

> "We loved with a love that was more than love"
>
> *Annabel Lee*
> by Edgar Allan Poe

OPPOSITE

*Silence Yourself:
Savages keeping the
gothic undead in
Berlin, 2013.*

LEFT

*PJ Harvey has two
Mercury prizes and
an MBE (Member
of the Most
Excellent Order of
the British Empire).
She has said she
possesses a "twisted
sense of beauty".*

OVERLEAF

*Sea Within a Sea:
Southend's finest,
The Horrors, met
through a shared
love of Bauhaus and
The Birthday Party.*

"It is important to look at death because it is a part of life. It is a sad thing, melancholic but romantic at the same time."

Alexander McQueen

FASHION

FASHION AND FANTASY are intrinsically linked. Forage deeply into dark gothic themes of love and death, and the potential for imaginative self-expression through fantasy costume is profuse. Visually elaborate and endlessly demanding of our attention, fashion's ongoing fascination with the mysterious romance of gothic horror has never been so ubiquitous.

In its broadest terms, gothic style provides a wealth of historical narrative with which to experiment, and there are so many incarnations of "gothic chic" to draw upon. It is a genre that has already been thoroughly examined by the fashion industry, yet the desire to revisit and playfully keep reinventing this theme with disturbing but decadent touches is more than apparent if we view the recent collections of international designers. It is testament to the visual diversity of a look, which appeals to both genders, that even today, more than 30 years after the original subculture appeared, you will still find a gaggle of black-clad Goths loitering around the back streets in most rural locations. The dramatic appeal of gothic as a means of visual communication has never waned

PREVIOUS PAGES

The master of macabre fashion, Alexander McQueen's Autumn/Winter 2001–2 collection "What A Merry-Go-Round" was inspired by the chilling 1922 silent movie Nosferatu.

because the idea of the angst-ridden teenager is not exclusive to any generation or geographical location. The solitary teen still exists all over the world, locked away in their bedroom, obsessed with a sense of gloomy foreboding and an unhealthy attraction to doomed romance. For many adolescents, a gothic identity, which typically prescribes a ghostly white face and lots of black velvet and lace, provides a perfect solution. It is a look that is immediately recognizable, one that stylistically draws on the macabre and makes a clear distinction between the wearer and the rest of the world. For anyone who wants to instantly show "outsider" credentials, this daily dress code of head-to-toe "black is back" provides immediate recognition.

In short it was in the early 1980s that gothic subculture evolved as a contemporary style that was easy to buy into through appropriate clothing. The cult of "Goth" that permeated globally became more dependent on a morbid fascination with horror than engaging in an intellectual gothic discourse. But the subculture and a finer intellectual examination of the subject have been embraced by contemporary designers on a cyclical basis, without repetition or cliché, and the wider framework of Goth has allowed numerous interpretations, from both haute couture and street-style designers.

The 1980s Origin of Goth

Like many other teenage subcultures, the original Goths evolved from the demise of an existing style tribe that was beginning to lose its authenticity. By 1981, the British punk scene had been superseded by the New Romantic movement, which in itself became increasingly acceptable in mainstream culture, permeating popular media through pop music, new magazines and fashion. Street-style fashion purposefully swings like a pendulum, blasting away what has become acceptable and clichéd and choosing instead to embrace what is predictably considered a polar opposite. In direct contrast to the cross-dressing, art-school Blitz kids, who were colourfully camp with their ruffled pirate shirts, knickerbockers and floppy hair, a select few, bored with this extravagant glamour, set upon the idea of finding something much more subversive. The darker aesthetic of gothic was seized upon. It cultivated a preoccupation with discordant thoughts, grotesque stories, romantic brooding and a general obsession with the darker side of life, all of which could be appropriated not only into a deathly look, but also a lifestyle.

In 1982, a new club called The Batcave opened in London's Dean Street, which was to have a major impact on transforming a small clique of the city's Goths into a much larger national movement. The club itself was almost a parody of everything gothic – black plastic bin bags stapled to the wall, a coffin-shaped entrance door and tatty spiderwebs glued across the ceiling and walls

**RIGHT AND
FAR RIGHT**
Individual Goth style successfully utilizes elements of other genres like punk in these two images taken at The Batcave, 1982 and 1984 respectively.

– but it attracted a crowd of like-minded souls. The Batcave legacy has been mythologized into the "birthplace of Goth", although it never claimed to be an exclusive Goth club. Perfectly located in the grimy back streets of Soho (think Dickensian London) and despite the fact that it operated only one night a week, it was a place for "otherworldly" outsiders to hang out and express individuality through fashion and music.

Since those very early days, Goth fashion has consisted of individuals creating their own version of the aesthetic. With the broadest of influences to draw on, from eternal darkness and haunting madness to monstrous creatures and vampiric fiction, there has never been a clear-cut style that distinguishes between individuals genuinely fixated on gothic themes and those who have latterly latched onto the genre and simply enjoy dressing up in some erotically charged *Rocky Horror Show* theatrical outfit.

For those who frequented The Batcave when it first opened, it was maybe enough to simply wear a profusion of black velvet with an exaggerated pale face and deathly black make-up. Youthful fashion exists through change and how much the Batcavers methodically embraced the deeper themes of melancholy is unclear. Outfits were often pulled together from a confusion of other styles, some of which were seized from the remnants of punk. There was only one rule: everything had to be black, with the exception of a flash of red or purple. Satin bodices, Victorian-style dresses, lace skirts, frilly gloves and fishnet tights were standard dressing-up items, either self-made or found in second-hand shops,

and the whole outfit was often completed with a leftover leather biker jacket. Goth hair and make-up typically relied on re-creating a *Night of the Living Dead* look, with porcelain skin, slashed bloodstained lips and inky dark pools of heavily made-up eyes. Hairstyles varied from post-punk spikes to longer, backcombed, femme fatale looks, but colour was not an option – invariably, both sexes dyed their hair a shade of ebony.

Costume jewellery fashioned to resemble imagery of dismembered body parts completed the look. Silver skulls, human skeletons and bats were worn hanging from silver chain necklaces or made into chunky rings, and brooches shaped as human bones were pinned onto dresses. Religious iconography in the form of ebony and jewelled crucifixes or rosary beads were draped around the neck, all sourced from vintage markets or bought from the shops of new young designers who recognized the emerging trend. The demand was growing among this young subculture for darker and more perverse clothing and jewellery. The gothic ideology and a wardrobe based on funereal black provided an extreme visual style that separated the defiantly moody teen from all that had gone before.

By the 1980s, Siouxsie Sioux, lead singer of Siouxsie and the Banshees, epitomized a post-punk gothic style that was much copied. Her spiky black hair, black eyeliner, applied into sweeping cat's eyes, and dark pouting mouth, as well as her strutting swagger, all conveyed the essence of modern Goth, but there were other bands who could lay claim to early gothic tendencies too, like Bauhaus, The Damned and Sisters of Mercy (see pages 128–73). These British bands sparked the germs of curiosity for an entire generation (and a male hairstyle has never been as copied as Robert Smith's from The Cure), but if the cult of Goth initially grew from street style in the UK, by the late 1980s there was a second generation of interest in Western Europe as well as the US. Inspired not only by the music scene, teens looked to cult movies, such as director Tim Burton's fantasy comedy film *Beetlejuice*. The 1988 film explored themes of horror, distinctly subversive behaviour and grotesque characterization in a lighthearted style, as did the much darker niche film of the 1990s *The Craft*.

Historical Fashion Influences

Much current gothic fashion is based on a somewhat arbitrary version of historical dress, and for many contemporary Goths it is enough to simply play the part of dressing up in costume that derives inspiration from the broadest of historical, literary and cinematic sources. They are able to draw from the romanticism of traditional medieval dress, the Victorian passion for elaborate black mourning dress, the elegant dandyism of nineteenth-century poets and the fragile beauty of the women portrayed in the paintings of the Pre-Raphaelites.

Traditional medieval dress, which is often referred to as "gothic fashion", is easy to identify primarily because of its strong silhouette. Women's gowns followed the lines of the body from shoulder to waist, with a long, full skirt attached to a bodice that flattened the chest like a corset. Two distinguishing details define this look and are often seized upon by modern Goths: dresses with a deep neckline in the shape of a low "V", to expose an expanse of décolletage (making them perfect vampire attire), and very long, exaggerated sleeves. These broadened out at the wrist into the shape of a bell and were, at times, so long that the bottom part of the hem touched the ground.

Gothic novels and poetry from the eighteenth and nineteenth centuries also provide an original source of authentic dress, but the gothic melodramas of the 1960s Hammer Horror films are equally influential (see pages 100–1). Although these provide kitsch parodies of the original gothic novel, they do inform current ways of dressing and have created a legacy of style that is appropriated by both male and female Goths.

Books like Mary Shelley's *Frankenstein,* Bram Stoker's *Dracula* and Arthur Conan Doyle's *Sherlock Holmes* stories are typical of gothic literature and provide a much more authoritative narrative on appropriate dress codes of the day. The dark stories that combine Romanticism with horror, and usually include a cast of mysterious characters inhabiting a twilight world of ghostly castles and shadowy graveyards, set the scene for villainous monsters, dashing heroes and women who are either evil bloodthirsty vampires or beautiful innocents.

The gloomy nature of these haunting stories dictates that Goth style should be predominantly black and based on Victorian clothing, but Goth's predilection for costume that creates artificial drama is, much like Frankenstein himself, often stitched together from disparate eras of fashion history. For most participants, style wins over substance, and the theatricality of the overall look is more important than historical accuracy.

ABOVE

The nostalgic view of the Victorian era as a period that merged romance and melancholy is epitomized in this portrait of Miss B – an unknown individual photographed by Gertrude Käsebier, c.1900.

OPPOSITE

A contemporary fetishistic Goth interpretation of Victoriana – complete with cameo brooch and decorative sash.

The Flamboyant Dandy

The English poet Lord Byron (1788–1824) and the great French literary figure Charles Baudelaire (1821–67) were both considered dandies, arbiters of a bohemian look that was defined by lifestyle as much as by attire. The dandy flaunted impeccable style credentials – a flawless frock coat, ruffled shirt with high collar, silk cravat and a tall, straight-sided stovepipe hat – but the term always conveyed less about wealth and status and more about attitude. For the contemporary male Goth, there are many elements of dandyism to covet. From a style perspective, the dashing flamboyance of the dandy, who paid obsessive attention to detailing and adorned himself with endless accessories such as white lace cravats, decorative cufflinks, pocket-watch chains, silver-topped canes and silk top hats, offers great scope for theatricality. Although the nineteenth-century dandies were not limited to a predominantly black colour palette, their style only needs to be reworked with gothic sensibilities to subvert it into something much darker and more sinister.

Although Byron gained notoriety for his writing, it was his troubled, solitary nature and dangerously complicated affairs of the heart that classify him as an iconic soul. He was the inspiration for an early example of vampire literature, written by his erstwhile friend John Polidori. *The Vampyre* (1819) was not the first type of story to deal with this subject matter but, unlike other tales of vampires, the protagonist, Lord Ruthven, was an educated, aristocratic monster who preyed on numerous young women, bringing evil into their lives. As the relationship between Byron and Polidori had already soured by the time this story was written, it was always presumed that the lurid, amoral Ruthven was, in fact, a thinly disguised Byron.

In classic literature, the mysterious figure of Heathcliff in Emily Brontë's *Wuthering Heights* (1847) exhibits similar character traits to those of the gothic Byronic hero. Portrayed as a dark-skinned gypsy, isolated from conventional society, he is a passionate outsider who stomps around the desolate countryside in breeches and boots, a fitted, black, three-quarter-length coat with silk scarf, revealing a white shirt collar and cuffs, exemplifying perfectly the idea of the tortured male, emotionally adrift. The look is the basis for many who dress up in gothic character today.

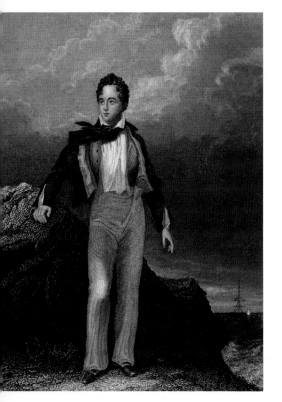

*Oscar Wilde,
one of the most
famous examples
of Dandyism,
exemplified as much
by an attitude as
by his extravagant
wardrobe.*

Victorian Medievalism

Portrait of a Young
Woman *by Hans
Memling, c.1480.
This classic medieval
painting depicts the
style of dress popular
in the Middle Ages.*

During the second half of the nineteenth century, a complex movement known as Victorian Medievalism evolved, which started to reference the Middle Ages in all aspects of society, art and architecture. At a time when English society was in the midst of social unrest and crippling poverty, there was clearly a cultural nostalgia for an era perceived as chivalrous and romantic. The Pre-Raphaelite Brotherhood, a group of seven English painters, including Dante Gabriel Rossetti and John William Waterhouse, developed a fascination with painting scenes that reflected life, albeit idealized, in medieval times. Famously, the Pre-Raphaelites produced many pictures of beautiful women with long, golden, crimped hair and fine complexions, dressed in jewel-coloured gowns. Their dresses were typical of the medieval style, with low, sweeping necklines and long, flowing sleeves.

These iconic portraits of beauty and innocence provide another source of gothic inspiration to inform current-day styling. The style of dress that the female Goth has appropriated most successfully, and which provides a continuing romantic escapism from our own twenty-first-century sartorial mediocrity, is that of formal Victorian mourning dress. At Goth conventions, you will find the majority of women, regardless of shape, size or age, head to toe in clothes that reference Victorian funerals. Black clothes were symbolic of spiritual darkness and were worn to convey a sense of sobriety and decorum. After Prince Albert died in 1861, Queen Victoria wore lavish mourning dress until her own death forty years later, setting the trend for other women to copy.

The fabrics used tended to be sumptuous velvet silk or satin, and the look, which was extremely decorative and elegant, reflected the fashionable trends of the period. Typically, a fitted jacket, cut to the waist and buttoning up to a high neckline, was usually trimmed with ornamental jet beads down the centre front and at the hem of the sleeves. This would be worn over a long, sweeping, hooped skirt that incorporated a small bustle, often with elaborate ruffled panels of stitched silk, heavily embossed

1 VICTORIA, THE WIDOW

After the death of her husband Prince Albert, Queen Victoria was only ever seen in black, starting the trend for elaborate and lengthy mourning periods. This illustration by Osbert Lancaster, c.1867, shows a bust of the late Consort standing on the steps beneath the queen's photograph.

with beads, frills or lace details. Any accessories had to complement the black dress, and it was commonplace to see women with black lace parasols, hand-held fans, purses, hair accessories and net veils – all in black. Modern-day Goths garbed in Victoriana sometimes wear head-hugging black bonnets, Little Bo Peep-style, with ribbon ties under the chin and a stiffened frill framing the face. Variations on a Mad Hatter top hat, usually adorned with decorative ribbon or feathers, are also popular for women, while men usually adopt the male version of the silk "topper" or stovepipe hat.

ABOVE

The Lady of Shallot *by John William Waterhouse,
1888. The Pre-Raphaelite painters were known for
their romantized view of tales from the Medieval Ages.*

OPPOSITE

*Anna Sui's Spring/Summer 2014 collection
clearly draws inspiration from the medievalism
as interpreted by the Pre-Raphaelite painters.*

Iconic Goths

Throughout modern history there have been certain characters that personify the very essence of Goth. With a combined sense of style and personality, they fuel the imagination for today's individuals to create their own gothic persona. The visual appearance of modern-day Goths of both sexes is open to interpretation, historically fluid and impossible to wholly define. Typically for men, the core elements of character would reference a turbulent relationship with love and a brooding melancholia, or perhaps a mysterious past that alludes to an unexplainable menacing darkness.

One of the first female movie stars hailed today as gothic inspiration is Theda Bara (1885–1955), the femme fatale of silent Hollywood films. At a time when the studio system deliberately chose to blur the lines between the real life and on-screen persona of its stars, Bara was forever known as a vamp. In the 1915 film *A Fool There Was,* she appeared as a man-hungry vampire, and the image remained with her throughout her short career. Her vampish look

was certainly dramatic. With naturally pale skin and thick black hair, she emphasized her eyes with heavy kohl and wore blood-red lipstick. Although Bara went on to play other roles, she has always been hailed as the original on-screen vamp and as such has become an iconic role model.

On the small screen, both Morticia Addams and Lily Munster, fictional characters in the American TV series *The Addams Family* and *The Munsters* respectively, which were both hugely popular in the 1960s, adopted the archetypal ghoulish look of medieval dress.

OPPOSITE

Theda Bara became famous as a sex siren in the early silent films of Hollywood. She mostly played the parts of alluring femme fatales and was nicknamed "The Vamp".

LEFT

Carolyn Jones in 1964 as Morticia Addams in the TV series The Addams Family.

Another flamboyant Goth girl was the Italian heiress Marchesa Luisa Casati (1881–1957). An extraordinary muse to the most influential artists of the time, such as Kees Van Dongen, Man Ray and Augustus John, she had a striking look. Her green flashing eyes were always heavily made up to dominate her face, and she switched her hair colour regularly between black and red. Her attitude to life and her obsession with extravagant fashion established her as a female dandy, while her wild behaviour, which included endless tortuous love affairs and outrageous antics – she was seen walking around Venice with a cheetah in tow, and used live snakes as necklaces – ensured fame as a femme fatale.

For wealthy women with a predilection for gothic styling, the genre provides ample imagery to fuel the imagination and many high-profile designers and collaborators who can encourage transformation. The European socialite Daphne Guinness who is usually recognized by her platinum hair streaked through with black (*Bride of Frankenstein* style) was a great friend and loyal fan of the late Lee McQueen and no-one embodies his signature style of dark glamour better than she does. Often seen in fierce black fetishistic leather she exaggerates her vampiric beauty and recently "played dead" in a macabre display of unworldly performance art. Dressed in a McQueen one piece, and beautiful antique veil she was laid out on a Perspex slab surrounded by candles in a fashionable townhouse in London to showcase an 18-carat diamond glove by the jewellery designer Shaun Leane.

OPPOSITE
Actress, model and socialite Marisa Berenson is dressed up to resemble Marchesa Luisa Casati at The Proust Ball in 1971 in this photograph by Cecil Beaton.

ABOVE
The wildly eccentric Italian Marchesa Luisa Casati Stampa, here photographed in 1900, had a reputation as a female dandy and maximized her vampish looks with extreme make-up.

A maverick dresser drawn to the darker side of international fashion fantasy, Daphne Guinness is known to channel a strong gothic aesthetic into her personal style.

English actress Helena Bonham Carter (married to the distinctly Goth-influenced director Tim Burton) is known for her eccentric style that combines elements of sultry vamp and Goth.

The gothic style of John Galliano's Autumn/Winter 2008 collection shown at Paris Fashion Week.

Goth Style: From High Street to Haute Couture

John Galliano's gothic chic was influenced by the British Victorian and Edwardian periods.

Inevitably, when the initial shock factor of 1980s Goth style waned and the look became watered down, a sanitized and stereotypical version of Goth appeared on the high street. But haute couture designers have let the emotional drama of such bleak imagery fuel their imaginations to produce the most beautiful creations. The themes of romantic Victorian gothic have proved to be an enduring and on-going source of inspiration, and designers regularly send their own interpretation of gothic chic sashaying down the catwalks.

For designers who like to immerse themselves fully in extensive research on a specific historical era, the gothic themes of purity and evil, lightness and darkness, and devils and angels provide a powerful starting point from which to begin a collection. Today there is an acceptance that gothic fashion is somewhat hybrid in its eclectic choices, and that participants often pick pieces from both historical and modern-day sources to provide references for their own interpretation, which has surely helped broaden the appeal. It is a fashion genre that has gathered followers from around the world, all of whom feel able to connect stylistically to the themes, but also to distort them freely. Despite these contrasting juxtapositions of past and present styles, it is important to acknowledge that, at its very best, a look based upon a romantic obsession with beauty and horror still has the capacity to fascinate.

Fashion designers at all levels often conceive ideas for collections based on different characters and identities, both real and fictitious. The drama of gothic literature provides a perfect platform to subvert the negativity of horror and death into something spectacularly beautiful. Gothic will inspire the design of dresses that reference dead and decaying flowers and use black as a default colour, ripping and shredding fine transparent organza, net and lace, to provide something visually edgy as well as stunning. Even macabre ideas like dripping blood can be re-presented to us as romantic destruction and reinterpreted as a tactile, blood-red print running down a black dress.

For designers like John Galliano and Karl Lagerfeld for Chanel, both of whom have referenced gothic influences, copious amounts of historical fact-finding will inform their work and ignite the first spark, to create a coherent theme for the season. From an initial body of research, they then allow their creative imagination to take flight and the detailed accuracy of historical notes can be marginalized in favour of extravagant fantasy presented for modern women. Galliano's slinky cobweb dress from Spring/Summer 1996 and, more recently, Christopher Kane's delicate black lace cobweb-style gown from Spring/Summer 2013 are both sourced from dark, mysterious imagery that is transformed by exquisite execution.

RIGHT
Visually stunning black leather and lace utilized by Jean Paul Gaultier Haute Couture Spring/Summer 2009.

OPPOSITE
The ultimate catwalk finale of black wedding dress by Jean Paul Gaultier for Autumn/Winter 2009–10.

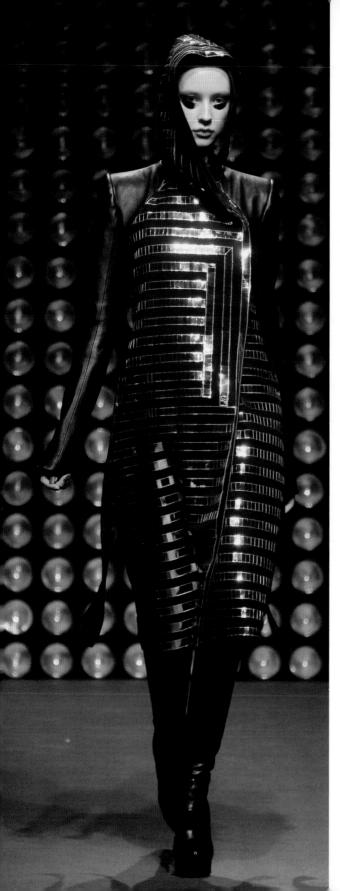

Themes of gothic art and literature have inspired many others, including Vivienne Westwood, Jean Paul Gaultier, Gareth Pugh and Giles Deacon, as the tension between earthly love and spiritual death provides huge potential to create fantastical fashion with a heightened sense of drama. Riccardo Tisci at Givenchy has a reputation for being a passionate Italian who favours darkly romantic heroines. For Autumn/Winter 2011–2, his almost all-black collection was sexy and chic with a definite nod to Goth, with models wearing pull-on black hats with little cat ears. The Japanese designers Yohji Yamamoto, Rei Kawakubo and Hirooka Naoto have all been known to produce collections based solely on a black colour palette, referencing the sombre darkness of gothic gloom – either through medieval touches, like voluminous sleeves, or Victoriana, with severe, high necklines and swathes of fabric draped bustle-like around the bottom.

OPPOSITE

An exaggerated silhouette and a severe shape defines Gareth Pugh's fashion work, which predominantly favours an all-black colour palette, from his Autumn/Winter 2012–13 collection.

LEFT

Black and gold leather dress as modern medieval armour by Gareth Pugh.

Alexander McQueen once said, "Death is part of life" and, of all the fashion designers, it was McQueen that was known for being drawn towards the more sinister side of life. Bizarre animal skulls and evil-looking birds are standard McQueen imagery, and his use of luxurious blood-red against melancholy black is a colour palette often repeated. As a designer, McQueen acknowledged his attraction to the contrasting relationship between heaven and hell, victim and aggressor. His posthumous collection for Autumn/Winter 2011–2, which included short bustle dresses cut from heavy black silk and dresses made from contrasting textures of fur and leather, cut up and restitched as if by a "mad scientist", was titled "Romantic Gothic". The Victorian tradition of taking a lock of hair from the deceased and wearing it in a locket was also appropriated by McQueen. In the days before his label became a global brand, he used to cut a lock of his own hair and stitch it into a see-though label on his clothes as a recognizable McQueen signature.

ABOVE
The late Lee McQueen was known for producing spectacular theatrical experiences to showcase the elaborate narrative of each collection, as here with "Joan" Autumn/Winter 1998–99

RIGHT

"The Horn of Plenty" Autumn/ Winter 2009–10. Subversive, sinister and obsessed with the dark side of life, the collections of Alexander McQueen were endlessly influenced by gothic literature and art.

LEFT

The designer Anna Sui often references gothic imagery within her collections, here for Autumn/Winter 1997–98.

RIGHT

Givenchy's creative director, the Italian Riccardo Tisci, has gained a reputation for collections that show romantic gothic touches. Autumn/Winter 2011–12.

The designer Anna Sui is another who has playfully incorporated elements of gothic as an integral part of her design ethos. Though never seriously sombre, her signature style often incorporates black lace, sequins, beading and embellished clothing, to produce a hybrid "sexy rock chic meets gothic stranger" style. This is a theme Sui returns to often and is one that her fans are familiar with – her perfume and make-up range is presented in shiny lacquered packaging adorned with black roses.

At the other end of the fashion scale, the term "gothic" has been repeatedly hijacked by advertising copywriters as a mainstream fashion term. In this commonly diluted sense, it is used primarily to reference a myriad of black party dresses that may or may not include lace or fishnet detailing.

Gothic Mutations

The rich diversity of contemporary Goth has spawned many offshoots as fashion continually responds to social and cultural change. Over time, the original look has mutated into other subgenres, which draw on different sources of inspiration and emphasize other aspects of style. These looks owe more to "cosplay", defined as a desire to dress up and play-act a part through specific costume, rather than an affinity to the roots of gothic art and literature.

Cyber Goth is a futuristic subculture that came out of the rave scene of the 1990s, merging "Goths" and "ravers" to create "gravers". The look is akin to urban disco, mixing elements from downtown New York warehouse raves with flashes of bright fluorescent Day-Glo, appropriated from the acid house scene in Britain. Black still underpins the Cyber Goth look, which favours PVC or rubber materials, but one contrasting neon shade – acid-pink or fluorescent orange – is usually incorporated for extravagant fake nylon dreadlocks, minuscule hot pants, chokers or wristbands. Fishnet tights and 5-inch black platform boots are obligatory, and the look is often accessorized with industrial-type aviator goggles or even gasmasks.

Gothic Lolita, known as GothLoli, is a hybrid street style most commonly seen in Japan, which combines the sweet girly innocence of Lolita fashion with Goth. The look is vaguely Victorian but not convincingly so, and there is much in the styling that is derived from an imaginary view of history. The style is demure with high necklines and mini-crini hoop skirts with black tights and chunky brogues or ankle boots. The pretty aspect is cultivated by wearing corsets with ribbons and bows, mini capes with ruffles and frills, lacy tights and gloves, and decorative accessories for the hair. Black dominates colour-wise but is often offset with white, pale pink or electric blue.

Fetish Goth can be connected to the predatory nature of Dracula and female vampiric style. It tends to be a darker type of cosplay, exemplified by an overtly sexualized dress code, that contains elements of Halloween dress. While costumes veer towards kinky, it is a genre based more on flirtatious dressing-up than sexual behaviour. Exhibitionist costumes of black PVC and rubber with bondage straps and collars suggest role-play of victim and aggressor. Shiny Lycra corsets and basques tied up with red ribbon laces, leather skirts, fishnet tights, chokers with crucifix imagery and vials of "blood" hanging from necklaces are standard uniform.

TOP

The Cyber Goth subverts the genre into an artificial future, taking elements of a gothic past and inverting with hair extensions and dance music.

RIGHT

Lolita Goth is a hybrid style that draws on elements from typical dark and gloomy traits combined with childlike styling.

In 1994 the seaside town of Whitby in North Yorkshire, England, held the first Gothic Weekend in a location that was associated with Bram Stoker's 1897 novel Dracula. *Now a bi-annual event, it has also spawned the annual World Goth Day on 22 May. Inspiration for dressing up at the event comes from many sources, like Tim Burton's movie* Edward Scissorhands *(top) but participants from every subgenre including Steampunk and Geisha Goth (right) are represented.*

INDEX

Page numbers in *italic* refer to illustration captions.

PICTURE CREDITS

The publishers would like to thank the following sources for their kind permission to reproduce the pictures in this book.

Key

t = top

b = bottom

l = left

r = right

Page 1 Francois Guillot/Getty Images; **2** The Kobal Collection; **4** akg-images; **7** Apic/Getty Images; **9** André Held/akg-images; **10** Hulton Archive/Getty Images; **12-13** Wikimedia Commons; **14** Musée Condé, Chantilly, France/Bridgeman Images; **15** Hervé Champollion/akg-images; **16l** Brian Jannsen/Alamy; **16r** Quagga Media UG/akg-images; **17** John Kellerman/Alamy; **18** Jon Arnold Images Ltd/Alamy; **19** Getty Images; **20** London Aerial Photo Library/Corbis; **21t** Angelo Hornak/Corbis; **21b** Andrew N. Gagg/Alamy; **22** Universal Images Group/Getty Images; **23** Westend61 GmbH/Alamy; **24t** Hervé Champollion/akg-images; **24b** Mim Friday/Alamy; **25** Franz-Marc Frei/Corbis; **26** Adam Woolfitt/Corbis; **27** Victoria & Albert Museum, London, UK/Bridgeman Images; **28-29t** Steve Back/Rex Features; **28b** © Victoria and Albert Museum, London; **29b** © Victoria and Albert Museum, London; **30** Houses of Parliament, Westminster, London, UK/Bridgeman Images; **31t** Mark Boulton/Alamy; **31b** Houses of Parliament, Westminster, London, UK/Bridgeman Images; **32** Superstock; **33** Steven Dahlman/Superstock; **34-35** The Gallery Collection/Corbis; **36** The Bridgeman Art Library/Getty Images; **37** Robert Harding Picture Library/Superstock; **38** Robert Harding World Imagery/Alamy; **39** Heritage Images/Getty Images; **40** The Gallery Collection/Corbis; **41** Brooklyn Museum of Art, New York, USA/Gift of William Augustus White/Bridgeman Images; **42** Philadelphia Museum of Art, Pennsylvania, PA, USA/Gift (by exchange) of Mr. and Mrs. James P. Magill, 1997/Bridgeman Images; **43** © Sarah Lucas, courtesy of Sadie Coles Gallery; **44** Courtesy of Olaf Breuning and Galerie Nicola von Senger, Zürich; **45** David Altmejd; **46-47** © Jake and Dinos Chapman, Photo by Stephen White, courtesy White Cube; **49** Matthew Barney/Tate, London; **50** Moviestore collection Ltd/Alamy; **51** Musée d'Art Contemporain de Montréal. Photo by Marcus Schneider, © The Easton Foundation/DACS; **52-53** Private Collection/Photo © Chris Beetles Ltd, London/Bridgeman Images; **54** British Library/Robana/Getty Images; **55** Fortean/TopFoto; **56** Mary Evans Picture Library/Alamy; **57l** akg-images; **57r** Private Collection/Archives Charmet/Bridgeman Images; **58** TopFoto; **59** akg-images; **60** Mary Evans Picture Library/Alamy; **61** Private Collection/Photo © Whitford & Hughes, London, UK/Bridgeman Images; **62** GL Archive/Alamy; **63** The Art Archive/Alamy; **64l** Wikimedia Commons; **64r** Photos 12/Alamy; **65l** Mary Evans Picture Library; **65r** British Library/Robana/Getty Images; **66l** Classic Image/Alamy; **66r** Culture Club/Getty Images; **67** Lebrecht Music and Arts Photo Library/Alamy; **68** Pictorial Press Ltd/Alamy; **69** Epic/Mary Evans Picture Library; **70l** Private Collection/The Stapleton Collection/Bridgeman Images; **70r** British Library/Robana/Getty Images; **71** North Wind Picture Archives/Alamy; **72-73** akg-images; **73** British Library/akg-images; **75** Transcendental Graphics/Getty Images; **76t** Private Collection; **76b** Harry Myers/Rex Features; **77** Bryce Lankard/Getty Images; **78** Raymond Kleboe/Getty Images; **79t** Mark Kauffman/Getty Images; **79b** PackStock/Alamy; **80** Mykel Nicolaou/Rex Features; **81l** PackStock/Alamy; **81r** Ben Molyneux/Alamy; **82-83** The Kobal Collection;

84 The Kobal Collection; 85 The Kobal Collection; 86 The Kobal Collection; 88 The Kobal Collection; 89t The Kobal Collection; 89b The Kobal Collection; 90 The Kobal Collection; 91 The Kobal Collection; 93 The Kobal Collection; 94t The Kobal Collection; 94b The Kobal Collection; 95 The Kobal Collection; 96 The Kobal Collection; 98 The Kobal Collection; 99 The Kobal Collection; 100 The Kobal Collection; 101 The Kobal Collection; 102 The Kobal Collection; 103 The Kobal Collection; 104 The Kobal Collection; 105l Private Collection; 105r The Kobal Collection; 106 The Kobal Collection; 107 The Kobal Collection; 108 The Kobal Collection; 109 The Kobal Collection; 110 Twentieth Century Fox Film/Sunset Boulevard/Corbis; 111 The Kobal Collection; 112 The Kobal Collection; 113 The Kobal Collection; 114 The Kobal Collection; 115 The Kobal Collection; 116-117 The Kobal Collection; 118 Pictorial Press Ltd/Alamy; 119 The Kobal Collection; 120 The Kobal Collection; 121 The Kobal Collection; 122 The Kobal Collection; 123 The Kobal Collection; 124 The Kobal Collection; 125 The Kobal Collection; 126 The Kobal Collection; 127 The Kobal Collection; 128-129 Rob Verhorst/Getty Images; 131 Kevin Cummins/Getty Images; 132 David Montgomery/Getty Images; 133 Pictorial Press Ltd/Alamy; 135 ITV/Rex Features; 136 Gijsbert Hanekroot/Getty Images; 138 Mick Hutson/Getty Images; 139 Michael Ochs Archives/Getty Images; 140 Michael Ochs Archives/Getty Images; 141 Everett Collection/Rex Features; 142t Jorgen Angel/Getty Images; 142b Jeff Morgan 11/Alamy; 143 Gijsbert Hanekroot/Getty Images; 144 Michael Ochs Archives/Getty Images; 145 Michael Ochs Archives/Getty Images; 146 Peter Still/Getty Images; 147 Ian Dickson/Getty Images; 148 Steve Richards/Rex Features; 149 Pictorial Press Ltd/Alamy; 151 Andy Freeberg/Getty Images; 152 Fin Costello/Getty Images; 153 Private collection; 154 Fin Costello/Getty Images; 157 ITV/Rex Features; 158 Martyn Goodacre/Getty Images; 159 Brian Rasic/Rex Features; 161t Photoshot/Getty Images; 161b Julian Broad/Contour by Getty Images; 162 Erica Echenberg/Getty Images; 163 ITV/Rex Features; 165 Mick Hutson/Getty Images; 166 Morven/Wikimedia Commons; 167 Mick Hutson/Getty Images; 169 Rankin/Trunk Archive; 170 Stefan Hoederath/Getty Images; 171 Jim Dyson/Getty Images; 172-173 Dean Chalkley/PYMCA/Rex Features; 174-175 Fairchild Photo Service/Condé Nast/Corbis; 176 Ted Polhemus/PYMCA; 177 Hartnett/PYMCA; 178l Derrick Ridges Photography; 178r Derrick Ridges Photography; 179l Derrick Ridges Photography; 179r Derrick Ridges Photography; 180 Sheila Rock/Rex Features; 181 The Kobal Collection; 182 Corbis; 183 Christina Simons/Corbis; 184 akg-images; 185 The Library of Congress; 186 TopFoto; 187 Karl Prouse/Catwalking/Getty Images; 188 Wikimedia Commons; 189 Hulton Archive/Getty Images; 190 Universal History Archive/Getty Images; 191 The Bridgeman Art Library/Getty Images; 192 © Tate, London; 193 Pixelformula/Sipa/Rex Features; 194 Everett Collection/Rex Features; 195 SNAP/Rex Features; 196 Condé Nast Archive/Corbis; 197 Mondadori/Getty Images; 198 Cindy Ord/Getty Images; 199 Kristian Dowling/AP/Press Association Images; 200 Getty Images; 201 Getty Images; 202 Sipa Press/Rex Features; 203 Frederic Bukajlo/ABACA/Press Association Images; 204 Antonio de Moraes Barros/Getty Images; 205 Antonio de Moraes Barros/Getty Images; 206 Paul Vicente/Getty Images; 207 Fairchild Photo Service/Condé Nast/Corbis; 208 First View; 209 Jacques Brinon/AP/Press Association Images; 210 Eric Charles/PYMCA; 211t Eric Charles/PYMCA; 211b Francisca Pinochet/PYMCA; 212t Ian Forsyth/Getty Images; 212b Darryl Gill/Alamy; 213 Nigel Roddis/Reuters.

Every effort has been made to acknowledge correctly and contact the source and/or copyright holder of each picture and Carlton Books Limited apologises for any unintentional errors or omissions, which will be, corrected in future editions of this book.